Glacier–
Waterton
International Peace Park

Glacier–Waterton
International Peace Park

SECOND EDITION

Vicky Spring
Photos by Tom Kirkendall & Vicky Spring

THE MOUNTAINEERS BOOKS

Published by
The Mountaineers Books
1001 SW Klickitat Way, Suite 201
Seattle, WA 98134

First edition, 1994; second edition, 2003.

Published simultaneously in Great Britain by Cordee, 3a DeMontfort Street, Leicester, England, LE1 7HD

Manufactured in Canada

Project Editor: Christine Clifton-Thornton
Editor: Karen Parkin
Cover and Book Design: Ani Rucki
Layout: Marge Mueller, Gray Mouse Graphics
Mapmaker: Tom Kirkendall
Photographer: Kirkendall/Spring
Cover photograph: *Beargrass in Swiftcurrent valley*
Frontispiece: *Aster Falls in the Two Medicine area of Glacier National Park (Hike 21)*

Library of Congress Cataloging-in-Publication Data

Spring, Vicky, 1953-
  Waterton-Glacier International Peace Park / by Vicky Spring ; photos by Vicky Spring and Tom Kirkendall.
       p. cm.
  Rev. ed. of: Glacier National Park and Waterton Lakes National Park.
  c1994.
  Includes bibliographical references (p.) and index.
  ISBN 0-89886-805-X (pbk.)
  1. Outdoor recreation—Montana—Glacier National Park—Guidebooks. 2. Outdoor recreation—Alberta—Waterton Lakes National Park—Guidebooks. 3. Outdoor recreation—Waterton-Glacier International Peace Park (Mont. and Alta.)—Guidebooks. 4. Glacier National Park (Mont.)—Guidebooks. 5. Waterton Lakes National Park (Alta.)—Guidebooks. 6. Waterton-Glacier International Peace Park (Mont. and Alta.) I. Kirkendall, Tom. II. Spring, Vicky, 1953- Glacier National Park and Waterton Lakes National Park. III. Title.
  GV191.42.M9S67 2003
  978.6'52—dc21
                                                                        2003001333

 Printed on recycled paper

Contents

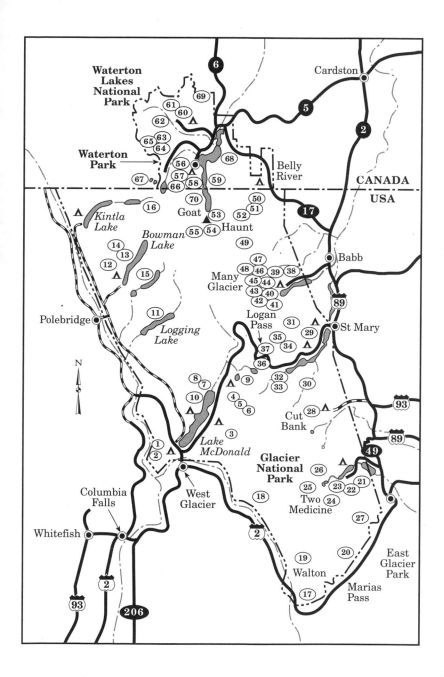

MAP KEY

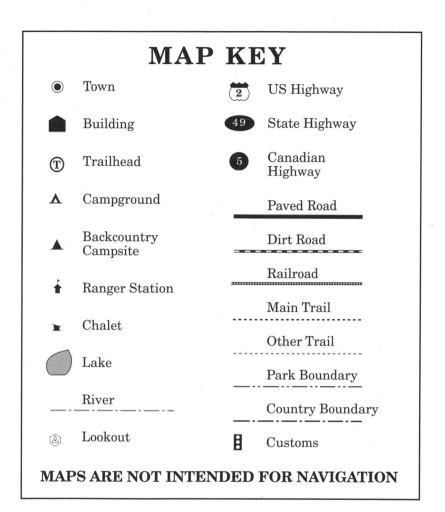

◉	Town	(2)	US Highway
⬟	Building	49	State Highway
Ⓣ	Trailhead	5	Canadian Highway
⚑	Campground		Paved Road
▲	Backcountry Campsite		Dirt Road
⚑	Ranger Station		Railroad
⌐	Chalet		Main Trail
⬮	Lake		Other Trail
	River		Park Boundary
Ⓐ	Lookout		Country Boundary
		⌷	Customs

MAPS ARE NOT INTENDED FOR NAVIGATION

Iceberg Lake at the base of Iceberg Peak in the Many Glacier area of Glacier National Park (Hike 46)

Introduction

In 1932 Waterton Lakes National Park in Alberta and Glacier National Park in Montana were joined together in the world's first International Peace Park to symbolize and give recognition to the cooperation and friendship between Canada and the United States. However, this was more than just a political union: the park also was created in recognition that the rare and delicate ecosystem of the northern Rockies does not end at arbitrary political boundaries.

Waterton/Glacier International Peace Park World Heritage Site has set a standard for the rest of the world. The formation of Waterton/Glacier International Peace Park was done in an astute manner that has encouraged the administrators of the two parks to work together and, at the same time, retain each park's unique cultural identity. The result is as we see today, two independent parks that share a common goal of preserving a single ecosystem from encroachments such as logging, mining, amusement parks, and overuse. The parks' administrators collaborate in the important areas of wildlife management, resource protection, fire suppression, environmental education, visitor communication, and transportation.

Despite the close ties between the parks, visitors must pay two separate entrance fees and follow two slightly different sets of rules. Visitors who cross the international boundary in either direction will notice enough cultural and philosophical differences between the two parks to enable them to savor the subtle thrill of visiting a foreign country.

GEOLOGY

The formation of the area we now know as Waterton/Glacier International Peace Park began sometime between 1,600 million and 800 million years ago. At that time the area was covered with a shallow sea. To the north, east, and south were highlands. Rivers carried sediments from the highlands to the sea, where, after millions of years of accumulation, rocks were formed. The beautiful red and green rocks found in both parks are the result of their watery origins. Ripple marks and fossilized algae that lived in the shallow sea bottoms can be seen in some formations.

Then, around 160 million years ago, the crustal plates along the western edge of the North American continent collided, resulting in buckling and folding of the land. A mountain chain rose out of the old seabed to form what is today the Rockies. It was an amazing, and extremely slow, process that lasted almost

100 million years. Great hunks of the earth were folded, contorted, and shattered. Huge masses of hard, old rock were shoved up and over much younger and softer rocks. The Lewis Overthrust, viewed from the Chief Mountain International Highway in Waterton Lakes National Park, is an example of 600-million-year-old strata overlaying 100-million-year-old strata.

When the growth phase ended, around 60 million years ago, erosion became the major force shaping this area. The tall mountains became rounded, and rivers cut broad valleys.

It was not until the Ice Age, just two million years ago, that this area underwent the transformation that sculpted it to the shape we are familiar with today. Huge rivers of ice filled the valleys and flowed down to the plains, carving the knife-edged ridges called *arêtes* (the Garden Wall is an example), the horn-shaped mountains (such as Clements Mountain), and the deep U-shaped valleys (such as the upper McDonald Creek valley).

Goat Lake lies in a glacier-carved valley below Avion Ridge in Waterton Lakes National Park (Hike 61)

The Ice Age ended a mere 20,000 years ago, and the last of the massive valley glaciers disappeared from the northern Rockies a mere 12,000 years ago. Since that time the world has seen numerous climatic fluctuations. During the early 1800s cool temperatures prevailed and once more the glaciers grew, surging down the sides of the mountains. Then, around the mid-1800s, the glaciers began a retreat that is still going on today. All glaciers in Glacier National Park have shrunk since the 1860s, and some have completely disappeared. Currently Glacier National Park has only thirty-seven glaciers, and if conditions remain as they are now, in twenty more years all the glaciers will have disappeared. No glaciers remain in Waterton Lakes National Park.

A VERY BRIEF HISTORY

Study of the hundreds of archaeological sites in Waterton Lakes and Glacier Parks has shown that this area has been inhabited for at least 11,000 years. The rich habitat along the shores of the parks' many lakes made ideal dwelling places in the summer and fall. Plains Indians used this area for hunting and spiritual purposes.

Today the First Nation tribes are an important part of Waterton Lakes and Glacier Parks. The eastern boundary of Glacier National Park borders on Blackfeet Nation lands; the eastern boundary of Waterton Lakes National Park borders lands owned by the Blood Indians. The best places to learn more about their life and culture is at the Head-Smashed-In Buffalo Jump, a World Heritage Site located northeast of the town of Waterton Park, and at the excellent exhibits in the Museum of the Plains Indian in Browning, Montana. Also park campgrounds and lodges offer weekly campfire talks by either a Blackfoot or a Blood tribal member.

The first Europeans in the northern Rockies were fur trappers, traders, and missionaries, many of whom were associated with the Hudson's Bay Company. These early explorers were soon followed by miners, loggers, whiskey traders, and ranchers.

The first chronicled exploration of the Waterton Lakes area was made by Thomas Blakiston in 1858. He is attributed with naming the lakes in honor of an English naturalist, Charles Waterton. Glacier National Park was named by a senator who hoped to lure visitors to the park. Many of the prominent park features were named to promote tourism rather than for historical reasons.

At the turn of the century, owners of the Great Northern Railroad helped to popularize the parks, building large and stately hotels to house visitors. They also sponsored a system of seven chalets around the parks, and visitors were taken from chalet to chalet on horseback. In 1924 the era of the automobile tourist began here when the Going-to-the-Sun Road was opened. The chalet system lost popularity, and horses gave way to hikers.

Hiker on a forested trail to Lincoln Lake in the Lake McDonald area of Glacier National Park (Hike 3)

Waterton Lakes Forest Reserve was created in 1895; Glacier National Park was created in 1910. The International Peace Park was a concept developed jointly by the Rotarians of Alberta and Montana. Through their efforts legislation was passed in 1932 in both the Canadian Parliament and the U.S. Congress that allowed formation of the Waterton/Glacier International Peace Park.

Waterton/Glacier International Peace Park became a Biosphere Preserve in the late 1970s as part of a UNESCO program that protects examples of the world's ecosystems for scientific and research studies.

In 1995 Waterton/Glacier International Peace Park gained more recognition when it became a World Heritage Site. These sites are chosen for superlative natural phenomena, outstanding beauty, and wildlife conservation, and are preserved as some of the greatest treasures of the world.

GETTING TO THE PARKS—ALTERNATIVES TO DRIVING

If a drive to Waterton/Glacier International Peace Park does not appeal to you, consider two popular options: train or plane.

Train

The train means Amtrak. There are three stops in Glacier National Park: the East Glacier Park Station located on the east side of the park, the Essex Station located near Walton, and the West Glacier Park Station (formerly known as the Belton Station) at the southwest corner of the park.

Airplane

The closest major airports are located 130 miles (208 km) southeast of the parks, at Great Falls, Montana, and 200 miles (320 km) north of the parks, at Calgary, Alberta. Smaller airports with commercial flights are located in Kalispell, Montana, 30 miles (50 km) southwest of West Glacier, and at Lethbridge, Alberta, 75 miles (121 km) northeast of Waterton.

Rental cars are available at all airports and train stations. From May 15 to September 25, park concession buses meet trains at both the East Glacier Park and West Glacier Park Stations.

TRANSPORTATION IN THE PARKS

Once you are inside the parks, there are a number of ways to get around.

Driving

The roads in Waterton Lakes and Glacier Parks are narrow, winding two-laners built for aesthetics rather than for rapid transit. In midsummer, when the traffic is heaviest, a drive through the park can be a slow, nerve-wracking experience.

The most difficult road to drive is the very popular and immeasurably beautiful Going-to-the-Sun Road. The road, completed in 1924, is open during the summer months only. Although the opening date varies from year to year, visitors can usually cross Logan Pass by mid-June. The closing date is in late October or after the first major winter storm. The road is narrow and, in some areas, beginning to age. To reduce congestion on the Sun Road, as it is popularly known, no vehicle longer then 21 feet, including bumpers, or wider than 8 feet, including mirrors, is allowed over Logan Pass. The restrictions apply only to a 25-mile section of road, from Avalanche Creek Campground on the west side of Logan Pass to Sun Point on the east side. In 2004, park administrators plan to start reconstruction of the Going-to-the-Sun Road. At publication time there was no finalized plan concerning travel over Logan Pass during the reconstruction. Check the park website for the most up-to-date information (*www.nps.gov/glac/*).

Shuttles and Buses

Shuttles and buses offer viable alternatives to driving in Waterton Lakes and Glacier Parks. In Glacier National Park, shuttle buses travel from the Swiftcurrent Lodge at Many Glacier to St. Mary, then traverse the Going-to-the-Sun Road to West Glacier and back, three times a day from July 1 through Labor Day. Signs along the road note bus stops and times. The shuttles are especially convenient for hikers who want to spend part of the day hiking at Logan Pass or who would like to start their hike in one place and end it somewhere else.

Tour buses provide transportation from the train stations to the hotels and major destination points in Glacier National Park. A daily bus runs between the Glacier Park Lodge in East Glacier National Park and the Prince of Wales Hotel in Waterton Lakes National Park. The Red Buses offer one-way trips, round trips, and tours. For information and reservations, contact Glacier Park Reservations, 106 Cooperative Way, Suite 104, Kalispell, MT 59901; (406) 756-2444; *info@glacierparkinc.com.*

In Waterton Lakes National Park, a hikers' shuttle makes daily morning runs up the Akamina Parkway to Cameron Lake. Other destinations are available on request. For current schedules and fees check at the Information Centre at the edge of town, Tamarack Mall, or Waterton Lakes Lodge in Waterton Park townsite (officially called Waterton Park).

Bicycling

In Glacier National Park bicycles are allowed only on established roadways and bike paths. Wheeled vehicles (bicycles, scooters, or skates) are not permitted on hiking or horse trails. Bicycle use is also restricted on the Going-to-the-Sun Road. From June 15 through Labor Day, two sections of road are closed to bicycling from 11:00 A.M. to 4:00 P.M. These are the 7.4-mile section of road around Lake McDonald from Apgar Campground to Sprague Creek Campground and the 11.4-mile section of road along the Garden Wall from Logan Creek to Logan Pass.

For touring cyclists and pedestrians, Glacier National Park has set aside a

Cyclists at the 6,680-foot summit of Logan Pass on Going-to-the-Sun Road

limited number of campsites at Apgar, Fish Creek, Sprague Creek, Avalanche Creek, Rising Sun, and St. Mary campgrounds. Each site has a metal storage box for food and supplies. Site capacity is eight people, and a fee is charged per person.

Waterton Lakes National Park has four trails open to mountain bikes. Cyclists are also welcome on all paved roads. Riding a bicycle in bear country has its own special challenges. Bicyclists move rapidly along forest roads and trails, and the chances of surprising a bear are much greater than for slower-moving hikers. Remember to make as much noise as possible when rounding corners in the woods; yell, talk loudly, sing, or ring an obnoxiously loud bike bell. Stay away from areas where bears have been sighted.

WEATHER

When packing for a vacation in the Waterton Lakes and Glacier Parks area, take a little time to think about the weather. On a typical day in July and August, temperatures are in the high 70s F (mid-20s C) in the valleys and the mid-50s F (about 10 C) in the high country around Logan Pass. At night the temperatures drop to the low 40s F (about 5 C). Unfortunately, the weather is rarely "typical" in the mountains. Heat waves may settle in for weeks at a time during the summer, and temperatures can soar to the upper 90s F (nearly 40 C). Snow is equally possible. In 1992 at Apgar, Montana, the temperature reached 97 degrees F (36 C) on August 21 and a foot of snow covered the ground on August 23.

Come to the parks prepared for any kind of weather. Bring tee shirts and sunscreen for the warm days, but don't forget to pack a warm jacket, raincoat, hat, and mittens for the cold days.

WHEN TO VISIT

Summer in the Rocky Mountains of northern Montana and southern Alberta is very short. The winter snowpack often lingers in the mountains until mid-July. Winterlike weather is not unusual in September. Most trails melt out by mid-July, so it is best to join the crowds and visit the parks in July and August.

WHERE TO STAY

Campgrounds

For aesthetic and economic reasons, camping is the most popular form of lodging in the parks. During July and August, the eleven campgrounds in Glacier National Park and the three campgrounds in Waterton Lakes National Park begin filling up by midmorning. Reservations may be made up to five months in advance for Fish Creek Campground in the Lake McDonald area and St. Mary Campground on the east side. Sites at the remainder of the campgrounds are open on a first-come basis. In July and August most sites are taken by noon, and visitors who arrive late must look to the private campgrounds at the outskirts of the parks. To reserve a site at Glacier call (800) 365-CAMP.

Groups of eight to twenty-four people may stay in the group camps at Apgar, Many Glacier, St. Mary, and Two Medicine in Glacier National Park, and at Belly River Campground in Waterton Lakes National Park. Contact the Glacier National Park or Waterton Lakes National Park headquarters for information (see the Appendix: Useful Addresses section).

Park campgrounds provide running water, and some have flush toilets. Utility hookups are available only at Waterton Townsite Campground. The larger campgrounds have disposal stations. Campgrounds in Waterton Lakes National Park have cooking shelters with tables and woodstoves. The smaller campgrounds—Belly River in Waterton Lakes National Park, and Cut Bank, Kintla Lake, Bowman Lake, and Sprague Creek in Glacier National Park—are set up to accommodate tent campers only.

Campground opening dates are staggered from early May through mid-June. The campgrounds begin to close down right after the first weekend in September. Some are open to primitive camping until they are closed by snow. During the winter months, only St. Mary Campground and the Apgar Picnic Area in Glacier National Park and the Pass Creek Picnic Area in Waterton Lakes National Park are open for primitive camping.

Showers. After spending a week or so hiking around the park, most campers begin to search for a shower. In Glacier, showers are available at Rising Sun and Many Glacier. Shower tokens can be purchased at the camp stores. The Waterton Townsite Campground offers showers and hot water in the rest rooms. Showers are also available at most of the private camp areas around the perimeter of the parks.

Laundry facilities. Laundromats are located at West Glacier, St. Mary, Many Glacier, and the Waterton Park townsite.

Hotels and Motels

Glacier Park, Inc., operates all of the hotels and motels in Glacier National Park. Visitors who plan to come in July or August should make reservations by mid-February. For information and reservations contact Glacier Park, Inc., 106 Cooperative Way, Suite 104, Kalispell, MT 59901; *info@glacierparkinc.com.*

Alberta Tourism is extremely helpful in providing lodging information for Waterton Lakes National Park. Their toll-free number is (800) 661-1222. Web information is found at *parkscanada.pch.gc.ca/waterton* or *www.watertonchamber.com.* Visitors should reserve lodging by mid-February for the following summer.

Note: Although the Prince of Wales Hotel is in Waterton Lakes National Park, reservations must be made through Glacier Park, Inc.

Hostels

Hostels provide inexpensive accommodations for the budget traveler. The hostel in East Glacier National Park is open from May 1 to October 15 and is within easy walking distance of the train station. For further information, contact Brownies Grocery and Hostel, Box 229, East Glacier Park, MT 59434; (406) 226-4426. The hostel in Polebridge has no easy access whatsoever. Because accommodations in Polebridge are extremely limited, it is best to make reservations ahead of time; contact the North Fork Hostel, Box 1, Polebridge, MT 59928; (406) 888-5241. You can phone the Waterton Park International Hostel, open year round, at (888) 985-6343.

High Mountain Chalets

Located in high mountain meadows, the Sperry and Granite Park Chalets rank among the most exotic lodgings in Glacier National Park. The chalets are in reality mountain hotels for hikers. They traditionally open July 1 and close mid-September. If you are looking for cheap sleeps, the chalets are not the place.

Swiftcurrent Lake, Many Glacier Hotel, and Wynn Mountain in the Many Glacier area of Glacier National Park

Cook house and dining room at Sperry Chalet in the Lake McDonald area of Glacier National Park (Hike 6)

However, for comfortable lodging, excellent meals, and unforgettable locations, the chalets are unbeatable.

For reservations at Sperry Chalet, contact Belton Chalets, Inc., P.O. Box 188, West Glacier, MT 59936; (888) 345-2649; *www.ptinet.net/sperrychalet.* For Granite Park Chalet reservations contact Glacier Wilderness Guides, P.O. Box 330, West Glacier, MT 59936; (800) 521-7238; *www.glacierguides.com.*

DAY HIKING

This is the most popular activity in the parks. Day walks require only a minimum of planning. Bring a small daypack for the Ten Essentials (see the Backpacking section below). You also should carry a map, such as the park handouts or a topographical map. Because there is always a chance of encountering bears on the trail, it is best to walk in a group and talk, shout occasionally, or sing as you go. You may also wear or carry some kind of noise-making device such as a can of rocks or a walking stick with bells. (Bear bells may be purchased at most park stores, but there is some debate about their effectiveness.) For more information, see the Bears section.

Hiking season begins early in the parks. By May, visitors begin exploring the lowland forest trails. However, it is not until mid-June to early July that the winter snowpack has melted sufficiently to allow hikers into the high alpine backcountry. If you plan to hike the high country during the late spring, carry an ice ax and know how to use it.

BACKPACKING

Extended trips in the backcountry require a great deal of planning before you leave home. Pack the Ten Essentials (map, compass, flashlight, food, clothing, sunglasses, first-aid supplies, pocket knife, waterproof matches, and fire starter), then add cooking gear, a tent (bears tend to respect a structure more than a person lying out unprotected), and a sleeping bag. Open fires are not allowed at most backcountry camps, so carry a stove for cooking. Water in the backcountry should be either boiled or filtered or both. (Boil for three minutes before drinking to kill *Giardia* protozoa.)

In Glacier National Park, backpackers are required to carry a 25-foot piece of cord for hanging food out of bears' and other animals' reach. Each official backcountry campsite has a specially designated area for hanging food with a wire stretched between two trees to make the process easier. When traveling cross-country or hiking in early season before the campsites have been officially opened, you may be required to carry a park-supplied bearproof container. In Waterton Lakes, elevated platforms are provided, and a cord, while handy, is not required.

Backcountry permits are required for all overnight camping in Waterton/Glacier International Peace Park. Backpackers are required to camp in designated backcountry camp areas, except in the Nyack–Coal Creek Wilderness Camping Zone in Glacier National Park and in the Lineham Lakes Basin in Waterton Lakes National Park. Camping in the designated areas is limited to the number of sites available. Each camping area has several tent sites, a cooking area, an outhouse, and wire for hanging food and other items.

In Glacier National Park, backcountry use permits are issued at the following locations: Apgar Visitor Center, St. Mary Visitor Center, Two Medicine Ranger Station, and Many Glacier Ranger Station. Fifty percent of the backcountry campsites in any given area may be reserved ahead of time. You may mail in your reservation request starting in mid-April. There is a steep, nonrefundable reservation fee, so be very certain about your itinerary before you mail in your form. The remainder of the backcountry permits are given on a first-come basis and are available the day before the trip. A per-person, per-night fee is charged to everyone when the permits are picked up, even to those

Hiking through beargrass up Belly River valley to Helen Lake (Hike 50)

who have reserved their permit ahead of time. For the most current information go to the Glacier National Park website, *www.nps.gov/glac/*, and download the *Backcountry Camping Guide.*

In Waterton Lakes National Park, backcountry use permits are issued on the day of the trip only. The permits may be obtained at the Information Centre located on the east edge of Waterton Park townsite. A per-person fee is charged.

In both Glacier and Waterton Lakes, early season backpackers are often faced with large snow slopes at the passes. These snow slopes can be dangerous through mid-July and it is best to schedule your trip to avoid them. If you decide to travel during the early season, carry an ice ax and know how to use it. In some areas, the snow slopes linger on cliff faces and the only way past is to detour around. Trail bridges on the major rivers and streams are often not replaced until after the snowmelt, normally mid- to late June. Most of these rivers are too dangerous to ford during the runoff season. Follow the advice of the ranger who issues the backcountry use permits and stick to the lowlands in the early summer.

Guide Services

Glacier Wilderness Guides offers day trips and backpack trips into the Glacier backcountry. Camping equipment may be rented. For information, write Box 535, West Glacier, MT 59936, or call (800) 521-RAFT.

FISHING

No license is required to fish in Glacier National Park. The park produces a pamphlet detailing all fishing regulations. Pick up a copy from any ranger station or visitor center and read it before fishing. If you want to check out the information and regulations before your visit, you may download the pamphlet from the Glacier National Park website (see the Useful Addresses section) or request a copy through the mail.

The practice of stocking lakes in Glacier National Park ended when it was determined that the native fish populations were suffering. Therefore, fishing can be a challenging business. In the larger lakes, the fish are easiest to catch where the water is deepest, and boats or rafts are very helpful. Fishermen without watercraft are advised to hike to some of the smaller mountain lakes. For details and helpful hints, pick up Paul Hintzen's book *Fishing Glacier National Park*, published by the Glacier Natural History Association.

Fishing conditions in Waterton Lakes National Park are similar to those in Glacier National Park. The only major difference is that a license is required. These may be purchased at the Information Centre in the Waterton Park townsite.

Fishing St. Mary River at the upper end of St. Mary Lake (Hike 32)

Paddling a canoe is a fun way to explore Bowman and Kintla Lakes

BOATING AND WATER SPORTS

You may bring your own watercraft or rent one in Waterton Lakes and Glacier Parks. Boat launch ramps are located at McDonald, Bowman, Two Medicine, St. Mary, and Middle and Upper Waterton Lakes. Rental boats (canoes, rowboats, and motorboats) are available at McDonald, Two Medicine, Swiftcurrent, and Cameron Lakes.

Canoes and kayaks are popular for exploring the wilderness lakes and for cutting off miles to reach the high country. Bowman, McDonald, and Kintla Lakes have backcountry campsites where canoes and kayaks may be beached. Overnight stays at these sites require a backcountry use permit. Canoe carts are not permitted on backcountry trails.

All the large lakes in Waterton Lakes and Glacier Parks are subject to sudden high winds. Small boats such as canoes and kayaks should be used with caution. Stay close to shore and beach your boat when the wind-driven waves become too high for safe paddling. No small boats are allowed on Upper Waterton Lake.

HORSEBACK RIDING

In the Glacier National Park area, saddle horse rides are offered at Apgar Corral, Lake McDonald Corral, and Many Glacier Corral. In the Waterton Lakes National Park area, Alpine Stables offers horse rides and pack trips (by reservation only). Horse ride lengths vary from one hour to all day.

For details on riding in Glacier National Park, contact Glacier Park Outfitters, Inc., 8320 Hazel Avenue, Orangevale, CA 95662, from mid-September through mid-May, and at Many Glacier Stable, Box 295, Babb, MT 59411, during the rest of the year. For more information about Alpine Stables in Waterton Lakes National Park, write to P.O. Box 53, Waterton Park, AB T0K 2M0.

HYPOTHERMIA AND WEATHER-RELATED ISSUES

Summer season at Waterton Lakes and Glacier Parks is very short. Temperatures vary dramatically from day to day. Snowstorms, while not common, can occur throughout the summer. In the higher elevations, temperatures may drop below freezing at night. On the other hand, temperatures may reach 90 F (33 C) every day for several weeks.

Long day hikes and extended backpack trips require carrying of a wide variety of clothes. Hiking in cool, wet, windy conditions can result in a lowering of the core body temperature if the hiker is not prepared. This lowering of the body temperature is a serious condition called hypothermia, which initially manifests itself by a loss of judgment and coordination. The best way to avoid hypothermia is to don raingear and warm clothes before you become cold and wet. If you have the symptoms of hypothermia, you need to stop, set up camp, and warm up. Drinking warm liquids and crawling into a sleeping bag with someone else are the two best ways to get the body temperature back up to normal.

WATER AND WATER TREATMENT

Despite the pristine look of the lakes and streams in Waterton Lakes and Glacier Parks, many small microorganisms live in the water and are spread about in the feces of rodents and animals. One of the best known, *Giardia lamblia,* causes diarrhea and other unpleasant, flulike symptoms one to two weeks after ingestion. The best way to avoid this painful disease is to either boil your water for three minutes before drinking, use a commercial filter rated for *Giardia lamblia,* or use a chemical purification additive such as iodine that is effective against microorganisms.

HIKING WITH BEARS AND MOUNTAIN LIONS

Bears

At the mere mention of Waterton Lakes and Glacier Parks, the first thing that comes to mind for most people is the ferocious grizzly bear. The media have expounded and expanded on the testy temperament of the park grizzly bears, sensationalized each incident, and created an image of a huge monster whose bloodthirsty and unpredictable behavior is unequaled by any animal since the tyrannosaurs.

The reputation of the grizzlies has enchanted our love of the sensational and scared us silly at the same time. Many park visitors feel cheated if they do not see a grizzly in the park and, at the same time, are so frightened of the bears that they are afraid to get out of their cars except at the visitor centers.

If the idea of hiking or camping with bears is worrisome, consider some reassuring statistics. In 2001 an estimated 800 grizzly bears roamed the lower forty-eight states. Of these, 350 lived within the boundaries of Glacier National

Park. About 500 black bears—which people, from a distance, often confuse with grizzlies—also live in the park.

Because park visitors should remain bear-aware at all times, here are safety guidelines to follow.

Follow the Rules

When you enter the park, you will be given a brochure that lists sensible rules to help people and bears coexist. These rules include leaving a clean campsite, staying away from bears and all other wild animals, and, most important, storing food where animals cannot find it. If you follow these rules, you have a good chance of enjoying a safe vacation. If you ignore these rules, you or someone who comes along after you may have serious trouble.

Both Waterton Lakes and Glacier Parks supply backcountry hikers with even more thorough bear information. Before obtaining a backcountry use permit, all backpackers are required to watch an instructional video dealing with how to behave in bear country. The video details sensible rules, which, when followed, greatly reduce the chances of encountering a bear.

Make Noise

Bears do not like to be surprised, so the number-one rule is to make noise while walking on the trail. Besides talking, singing, and loudly clapping hands whenever you are walking near a stream, going around a corner, or passing through dense vegetation, carry some kind of constant noisemaker to take up the slack when the vocal cords need a rest. A pop can with a couple of rocks inside makes obnoxiously repellent noise, if you remember to shake it. Bear bells, if you don't mind dangling ten or so off your body, will make enough noise to drive you up the trail and hopefully keep the bears away. The best noisemakers are the creative ones: bicycle horns, whistles, castanets, or anything that makes a fairly loud and obnoxious sound work well to warn bears that a human is approaching.

Travel in Groups

For hikers and backpackers, the most effective way to avoid bear attacks is to travel in large, noisy groups. Several people singing off-key or arguing politics is more than a normal bear can stand. There are no known incidents of bears attacking parties with eight or more members who are hiking together. To stay safe the group must stick together on the trail, with no one going ahead or lingering at the end of the line!

Of course, there are people who value the peace and quiet of the wilderness more than they value their own lives or the lives of the bears. Before you join their ranks and take your chances, remember that most attacks on humans come from bears that were surprised and did not have time to move away before a hiker arrived.

Carry Bear Spray

Although avoidance is the best defense, many hikers carry cayenne pepper spray for self-protection. These "bear sprays" have proven to be quite effective.

However, both Glacier and Waterton Lakes are known for their windy weather, and you do not want to be downwind from a blast of pepper spray. Most hikers carry at least one can per group, and rangers also carry it. Pepper spray rules are simple: The bear must be no more than 15 feet from you before you use it, and do not attempt to spray into the wind. The spray can be purchased at camp stores within Glacier National Park and at the backcountry offices.

Avoid Creating a Scent

Bears are extremely intelligent. They not only remember where they once found food in a campground or picnic area, they also pass this information along to their offspring. To protect bears, park officials diligently patrol the parks looking for anyone who leaves coolers, food, or cooking paraphernalia where bears can find it.

Trailhead sign indicating that a bear has been sighted in the area

Keep backcountry meals simple and nonaromatic. Bears can smell cooking sausage and bacon for miles. Bland meals of rice, potatoes, or noodles and vegetables have little or no odor and will sustain life without creating the enticing smells that attract bears.

Backcountry campsites are set up so that cooking and sleeping areas are separated. If you plan to do any hiking in Glacier National Park, be sure and pack 25 feet of lightweight cord and a couple of sturdy stuff bags for hanging extra food, the clothes you cooked in, and any scented toiletries, such as toothbrush and toothpaste, sunscreen, and mosquito repellent. It is best to avoid using deodorants, cosmetics, and scented soaps when hiking or camping in bear country.

There has been a lot of speculation about whether it is safe for women to hike when they are menstruating and whether sexual activity can attract bears. To date there is no conclusive proof showing that either of these two situations precipitate bear attacks. However, it never hurts to err on the side of caution. Women hiking during menstruation are advised to carry used products in a plastic bag that has been partially filled with baking soda to cut the odor. Place this bag in one or two other strong bags and hang it with the food at night.

Bear tracks

Report Bear Sightings

To further protect yourself and other hikers from bears, be sure to report bear sightings to the ranger. If several sightings are made in the same area, the trail will be posted, warning other hikers of a possible bear encounter. If a bear acts aggressively, a bear expert will be sent out to investigate. If the situation is potentially serious, such as a sow with cubs, the trail may be closed to hikers until the bears move on.

Be Prepared

If you should encounter a bear on the trail, follow the rules listed in the park information handouts. Read the suggestions carefully, then devise your own action plan. Before you set out, review your plan with your hiking partners so everyone is ready. If hiking with children, remind them that the scariest thing about bear country is that they have to stick with their parents, staying in sight at all times; no running ahead or lagging behind.

Although you may be determined to reach your destination, allow some flexibility in your plans. If you encounter a bear on the trail, retreat and wait a half hour or more, giving it time to move on. If possible, you can retreat, then detour around the bear.

Mountain Lions

Although most park visitors are concerned about aggressive grizzly bears, there is a growing problem with mountain lions. The mountain lions, also known as cougars or pumas, were largely driven out or killed by the early settlers. Now these animals are making a comeback.

Mountain lions are clever hunters and rarely seen by park visitors. Occasionally their tracks are spotted, but even that is unusual. They tend to attack young children who weigh 100 pounds or less. The best defense against potential cougar attacks is for children to stay close to parents when hiking. Do not allow the kids to run ahead, out of sight of an adult. Do not allow one or several children to hike without adults.

If someone in your party is attacked by a mountain lion, you must act aggressively; beat it with a stick or rock, make loud noises, and if necessary force its mouth open. Do not act meek or attempt to play dead. Do not run for help. Act quickly, decisively, and with force.

LEAVE NO TRACE

When you join the thousands of hikers who annually explore the fragile backcountry of Waterton/Glacier International Peace Park, it is important to employ your best *No Trace* traveling and camping skills. The following are the seven principles of *No Trace* backcountry use.

1. Plan ahead with adequate food, clothing, and stove fuel for all possible conditions. Always be ready to spend an extra day or two waiting out bad weather.
2. Leave what you find and never make alterations to natural features or even preexisting campsites. Only berries and fish may be consumed.
3. Carry a campstove for your cooking. If fires are allowed, collect only dead wood found on the ground. Leave all wood that is larger than your wrist. Keep your fire small and totally contained in the fire pit.
4. Always camp and walk on durable surfaces. On the trail, walk single file down the center, even if the center is muddy. When off trail, avoid walking on the fragile vegetation; try to stay on rocks, gravel, dry grasses, or snow.
5. Pack out all litter. Use toilets when available. When no outhouse is near in

a time of need, dig a cat hole at least 6 inches deep and at least 200 feet from water sources. Urinate on rocks or other durable surfaces to avoid damage to vegetation by salt-craving wildlife such as mountain goats.

6. Never intentionally approach any wild animal. Go way around any wildlife found along the trail. Hang all food and odorous items unless you are in the process of using them. When photographing wild animals, use only a telephoto lens and always stay well back from them.

7. Backcountry campsites are small and facilities must be shared. Keep your noise down in camp and try to be friendly and considerate to fellow campers.

Group Size

The maximum group size for overnighting is limited to twelve people (with an eight-person capacity for each backcountry camping site). No more than four people in two small tents are allowed per tent site. Large groups, nine to twelve people, are advised to make advance reservations.

For More Information

For more information about park activities, contact the parks' headquarters. For Glacier National Park, contact the Park Superintendent, Glacier National Park, West Glacier, MT 59936; (406) 888-5441; *www.nps.gov/glac/*. For Waterton Lakes National Park, contact Waterton Lakes National Park, Waterton Park, AB T0K 2M0; (403) 859-2224. For Glacier TDD service, call (406) 888-5790.

THE GUIDE TO THE GUIDEBOOK

The hikes and backpacks described here are designed for the "average" person. This somewhat mythical being moves along the trail at a steady 2-miles-per-hour pace, a bit slower if the trail is very steep. Real-life hikers are not robots. Paces will vary with the amount of elevation gain and the strength of the group.

At-a-Glance Overview. The hikes in this book are organized by area. Each area has a basic introduction describing location, camping, and other services. Use the area Trail Finder to determine which hikes are of interest, then skip on to the description for a detailed discussion of the trail.

Information Block. At the top of each hike description is a list of all the important information about the hike—distance, elevation gain, high point, time needed to complete the hike, best months for the hike, difficulty of hike, type of hike, and maps needed. Once you have looked at this information and found that it fits your requirements, check out the text to determine if this is a location you want to visit.

Mileage. Each hike description begins with the total mileage. Most mileages are given for the round trip or loop trip from the trailhead and back again. A couple of hikes, such as the Continental Divide National Scenic Trail, are one-way trips and require transportation at each trailhead.

Elevation gain. The amount of elevation gained is listed next. The mileage combined with the elevation gain information will allow each hiker to choose whether the hike is appropriate for the time available and the strength of the group. Note that elevations are given in both feet and meters. For hikes in the U.S. the elevations are given in feet followed by the metric equivalent. Hikes in Canada have the metric elevation change listed first.

High point. This handy bit of information will help you decide when the hike will be snow free. Although this guidebook notes when the trail *should* be open, weather is totally capricious and the rate of snowmelt varies radically from year to year. Your best bet is to check with the park before setting out on a hike. In May, June, and early July park rangers can usually give you an estimation of the elevation where you will encounter the snow.

Hiking time. This is the average amount of time it takes most hikers to complete the hike, based on a 2-miles-per-hour pace. If the trail is very steep or difficult, extra time has been figured in. Hiking time is the time spent walking and does not include time for eating, fishing, swimming, exploring, napping, wildlife watching, or taking bear detours.

Hikeable. This category, along with the high point information, will help you determine when the hike most likely will be snow free. Another name for this category would be "Best guess." The amount of snowfall during the winter and the time it takes to melt varies from year to year. Hikers coming from long distances are advised to visit in August.

Difficulty. This is a nebulous category and should be treated as such. The trails in this book have been divided into four degrees of difficulty: easy, moderate, strenuous, and difficult. *Easy* trails have little elevation gain and work best for groups with varying energy levels. Most hikes in Waterton Lakes and Glacier Parks fall into the *moderate* category. *Moderate* hikes are on well-graded trails and may be accomplished in one day or as an easy backpack. *Strenuous* hikes are on steep and possibly poorly graded trails. These hikes are physically demanding and may require either experience or good sense to complete safely. Finally, there are a couple of hikes in this book rated as *difficult*. Inexperienced hikers should not attempt these hikes. Some of the challenges found on these *difficult* hikes include fording major rivers and routefinding on poorly maintained trails.

Day hike or backpack. At a quick glance you can check to see if you can turn the day hike into an overnight adventure.

Maps. Most trails in the park are well marked and easy to follow. However, if you should ever need to depart from the main trail to detour around a washout, a bear, or a dangerously steep snowfield, only a map can help you find your way back. Before starting out for a day of hiking it is critical to know where you are going. If one of your party should get sick, if the weather changes suddenly, or if someone in the group runs out of water, it is important to have a map that will help you determine where you are and whether you should go forward or turn around. Maps supplied by rangers at both Waterton Lakes and Glacier Parks are excellent resources. These maps will help you locate trails and trailheads. If you experience difficulties, you will need a topographical map showing the contours. Waterton Lakes National Park has a wonderful 1:50,000 contour map that covers the northern portion of Glacier National Park as well. In Glacier National Park, there are several good maps available at the park bookstores. The USGS Glacier National Park 1:100,000 scale covers the entire park and is good enough for most hikes, except those into the wilderness areas at the southern sections of the park, such as Hikes 18 and 20.

In the Maps section of each hike in Glacier National Park, there is a listing of the 1:24,000 contour maps for the hike. These maps offer the greatest detail and necessary equipment for off-trail travel and all emergency situations. A GPS (Global Positioning System) can also be a helpful device. Take the time to understand its uses and functions before you start your hike.

A NOTE ABOUT SAFETY

Safety is an important concern in all outdoor activities. No guidebook can alert you to every hazard or anticipate the limitations of every reader. Therefore, the descriptions of roads, trails, routes, and natural features in this book are not representations that a particular place or excursion will be safe for your party. When you follow any of the routes described in this book, you assume responsibility for your own safety. Under normal conditions, such excursions require the usual attention to traffic, road and trail conditions, weather, terrain, the capabilities of your party, and other factors. Keeping informed on current conditions and exercising common sense are the keys to a safe, enjoyable outing.

The Mountaineers Books

Part One

Glacier National Park

Lake McDonald

The largest of the 250 lakes in Glacier National Park is 11-mile-long Lake McDonald. It lies in a broad, glacier-carved valley surrounded by tree-covered hillsides that come to an abrupt end at a towering barrier of mountains known as the Garden Wall.

Lake McDonald serves as a staging area for visits to the park. The lake is located only a couple of miles off US Highway 2 and for many visitors this is their first glimpse of the park they may have traveled so far to see. Weather is mild around the lake, making it a great base for further explorations and a delightful place to return to after spending a day in the wind on the east side of the park.

The Lake McDonald area has three separate "hubs." The first is the town of West Glacier, located just outside the park boundary at the Highway 2 turnoff. Two miles east, inside the park, is Apgar Village, situated on the shores of the lake. The third hub is the Lake McDonald Lodge complex, located near the upper end of the lake, 9 miles east of Apgar.

Avalanche Creek in Avalanche Gorge

LAKE McDONALD TRAIL FINDER

Trail Number and Destination	Difficulty	Lowland Lakes	Alpine Lakes	Waterfalls	Scenic Views	Wildlife	Fishing	Backpacking
1 Trail of Cedars	easy			●				
1 Fish Lake	moderate	●						
1 Huckleberry Mountain Nature Loop	easy							
1 Rocky Point	easy	●				●	●	
1 Howe Lake	easy	●						
2 Apgar Lookout	moderate				●			
3 Lincoln Lake	moderate			●		●		●
4 Mount Brown Lookout	strenuous				●			
5 Snyder Lakes	moderate	●						●
6 Sperry Chalet	moderate			●	●			●
6 Gunsight Pass	strenuous						●	
6 Sperry Glacier	strenuous				●			
7 Sacred Dancing Cascade Loop	easy	●		●				
8 Trout and Arrow Lakes	moderate	●			●		●	●
9 Avalanche Lake	easy			●	●	●		
10 Lake McDonald Trail	easy	●			●		●	●

ACCOMMODATIONS AND SERVICES

In the Lake McDonald area, lodging is available both inside and outside the park. The most notable of the accommodations is regal Lake McDonald Lodge, which is actually a combination of a beautiful, stately old wooden hotel, a motel, and cabins. At Apgar Village there are two motels: the Village Inn Motel and the Apgar Village Lodge. There are also two motels in West Glacier and more lodging along Highway 2, west of the park. Most of the motels outside the park are in Columbia Falls, Kalispell, and Whitefish, a ski resort town 30 miles from West Glacier.

Campers have the choice of four campgrounds around Lake McDonald. Apgar Campground, near Apgar Village, has 196 sites, and nearby Fish Creek Campground has another 180 sites. Sprague Creek Campground, located near Lake McDonald Lodge, is a small, twenty-five-site area that caters to tents. The eighty-seven-site Avalanche Campground is located about 4 miles above the upper end of Lake McDonald, at the edge of a grove of large cedars and at the head of a popular trail to Avalanche Lake (Hike 9). Most campgrounds fill up by midmorning during the summer. Late arrivals must find spots in the private campgrounds west of the park entrance along Highway 2.

Evening programs, hosted by a park naturalist, are held nightly at Lake McDonald Lodge, Apgar Amphitheater, Avalanche Campground, and Fish Creek Campground. Program schedules are posted in the campgrounds, at Apgar Visitor Center, and at the lodge.

The town of West Glacier has three restaurants. Two miles away, at Apgar Village, there is a restaurant and a deli. At Lake McDonald Lodge, a formal dining room, a coffee shop, and a lounge serve guests and drop-ins.

Groceries, fishing gear, and camping supplies are available in West Glacier. The camp stores at Apgar and Lake McDonald Lodge offer only the most basic of food supplies. Tee shirts and souvenirs are available everywhere, with the largest concentration of gift shops at Apgar.

A Laundromat, a post office, a camera shop, a one-hour photo lab, an eighteen-hole golf course, and two gas stations are located in the town of West Glacier.

■ ■ ■ ■

1. LAKE McDONALD AREA SHORT HIKES

Some beautiful, some educational, and a couple of fun lowland lake strolls round out the available list of short trails in the Lake McDonald vicinity. If you only have time for one, make it the Trail of the Cedars. If you are on an extended stay, hike them all.

Trail of the Cedars. This is a 0.8-mile loop trip, through a grove of 500- to 700-year-old western red cedars. The trail passes through a garden of ferns and near weeping rocks. The high point of the loop is a view into the swirling waters of Avalanche Creek as it exits a deeply carved gorge. Due to the dampness of the area, nearly half the path is on a boardwalk, making the loop suitable for wheelchairs and strollers. The hike can be extended by following the trail on to Avalanche Lake (Hike 9). The trailhead is located 15.8 miles east of the West Glacier Entrance Station on the Going-to-the-Sun Road, just beyond Avalanche Creek Campground.

Fish Lake. This 4.8-mile round trip is an excellent afternoon workout for visitors at Lake McDonald Lodge. The trail is moderately difficult, climbing steeply and gaining 1,000 feet before arriving at the reedy lake. To reach the trailhead, follow the directions given in Hikes 4 through 7. Walk across the Going-to-the-Sun Road from Lake McDonald Lodge and head uphill on the Sperry Chalet Trail for 1.7 miles. Pass the junctions for Mount Brown Lookout and Snyder Lakes. After crossing Snyder Creek go right and walk along the ridge for the final 0.7 mile to the lake.

Huckleberry Mountain Nature Loop. This is a short and rugged 0.6-mile loop through a burn area. The loop offers the opportunity to see a forest in the process of regeneration and to compare it with an old-growth area. The trail begins 300 feet west of the Camas Entrance Station, 12 miles north of Apgar Village.

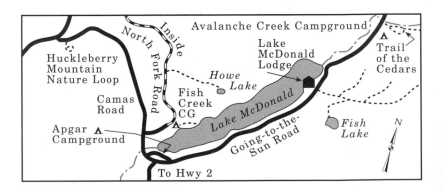

Hikers on the boardwalk along Trail of the Cedars

Rocky Point. An easy 2-mile round trip on a level trail leads to a viewpoint on the shores of Lake McDonald. The hike begins in the Fish Creek Campground or from the Inside North Fork Road and is an ideal morning or afternoon stroll for anyone staying there.

Howe Lake. This easy, 4-mile round trip gains only 240 feet on its way to a marshy lake in the forest. Moose are occasionally seen along the trail and at the lake. The hike begins 5.4 miles north of the Fish Creek Campground on the primitive Inside North Fork Road.

Waterton/Glacier International Peace Park is a kid-friendly place with a lot of activities to participate in.

WATER: Tour-boat rides on the major park lakes may be combined with hikes to create appealing day trips. Canoes can be rented at Lake McDonald, Two Medicine Lake, Shernborne Lake, and Cameron Lake.

WILDLIFE: For mountain goats, head to Hidden Lakes Overlook at Logan Pass. Bighorn sheep are frequently spotted along the Garden Wall and Piegan Pass Trails. For bears, plan a night at Many Glacier. In the evening the park naturalists set up spotting scopes in the store parking lot. For moose, the best bet is the easy backpack trip to Kootenai Lakes from Goat Haunt Ranger Station. In Waterton Lakes National Park, a herd of bison can be viewed from your car at the Buffalo Paddock.

THRILLING TRAILS: For the older kids, try one or more of the following hikes: Crypt Lake, the Garden Wall, and Ptarmigan Tunnel.

JUNIOR RANGER PROGRAM: Glacier National Park offers a Junior Ranger program for kids ages six through eleven. Children are given a packet of activities to choose from. After completing age-appropriate tasks, they receive a badge.

CAMPFIRE PROGRAMS: Most of the park naturalists go to great lengths to make sure their programs are as interesting for children as they are for adults. Children may be asked to participate in the presentation.

BICYCLING: Campground roads seem more like bicycle raceways than places for cars. If staying in the Apgar area, take advantage of the bicycle path down the valley to West Glacier.

HORSEBACK RIDES: Stables at Lake McDonald, Many Glacier, and Waterton Park offer guided horseback rides of various lengths.

■ ■ ■ ■

2. APGAR LOOKOUT

DAY HIKE
Round trip: 5.6 miles (9 km)
Elevation gain: 1,856 feet (566 m)
High point: 5,236 feet (1,596 m)
Hiking time: 3 hours
Hikeable: July through September
Difficulty: moderate
Map: USGS McGee Meadow

From the quiet wilderness of the Apgar Mountains, you can gaze out over the modern world, where high-tech rafters drift along the river, golfers buzz around immaculate greens in little white carts, trains ease out of a long series of tunnels and speed across the open valley, and a seemingly endless stream of motor vehicles zip in and out of the park.

This fascinating view is reached by a short, rather steep trail that climbs from the Middle Fork Flathead River valley to a fire lookout on the shoulder of the Apgar Mountains. Carry plenty of water, as none is available at the lookout, and wear sturdy shoes—the trail is coated with a layer of horse by-product.

Access: Drive from the West Glacier Entrance Station into the park for 0.3 mile, then turn left, following signs for "Trail Rides." The paved road ends at the stables. Continue straight ahead on a dirt road for 0.5 mile to McDonald Creek and the Quarter Circle Bridge. If your vehicle is not designed to tackle rocks and deep potholes, or if you would simply like to extend the hike, park just before the bridge. The

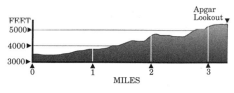

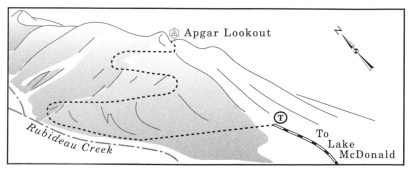

road continues on, paralleling the Middle Fork Flathead River. At the end of a mile the road divides. Go right for the final 0.5 mile to the parking area (elevation 3,380 feet).

The hike: Walk around the gate, then climb through forest following an old road for the first 0.8 mile. Once the trail leaves the road, it begins a steady climb toward the lookout. The views appear after the second switchback and continue to improve all the way to the summit.

The trail crests a ridge at 2.7 miles, then tunnels through high brush across a narrow saddle. A short, final climb leads to the lookout. Visitors may climb the lookout tower and wander around the balcony in search of views. If you carried a map, it's time to unfold it and identify the incredible panorama of summits extending from the park to the Flathead National Forest.

Middle Fork Flathead River valley viewed from Apgar Lookout

■ ■ ■ ■

3. LINCOLN LAKE

DAY HIKE OR BACKPACK
Round trip: 16 miles (25.6 km)
Elevation gain: 1,927 feet in; 480 feet out (587 m in; 146 m out)
High point: 4,880 feet (1,487 m)
Hiking time: 8 hours
Hikeable: July through September
Difficulty: moderate
Maps: USGS Lake McDonald West and Lake McDonald East

Located in a deep cirque, Lincoln Lake is fed by Beaver Chief Falls, an exotic waterfall with two parallel cascades streaming over the sheer cliff, creating a startlingly beautiful scene. With that stated, it must be admitted that the access through dense and viewless forest is less then inspiring. If nothing else the viewless approach insures a fuller appreciation of the lake when you arrive.

Access: Drive east from the town of West Glacier on Going-to-the-Sun Road for 9.5 miles. The trailhead is located in a turnout on the east side of the road (3,160 feet).

The hike: Wasting no time, the trail leaves the highway and heads uphill. Before long you will see the trail as a mirror of the terrain. When there is a level area, the trail is level. When the hillside climbs steeply, so does the trail—like a rocket.

After 1.7 miles and an elevation gain of 1,270 feet, the trail bisects the rarely traveled Snyder Ridge Fire Trail. You are granted a short respite before the climb resumes, at a reasonable pace now, heading for the 4,880-foot high point on a forested ridge. The trail

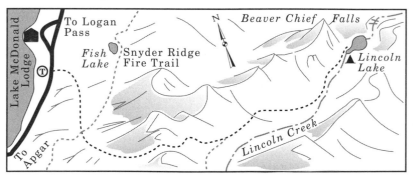

In July, beargrass brightens the forest along the trail to Lincoln Lake

then descends to Lincoln Creek. The descent is hesitant at first with a few ups, but soon settles into a steady drop, reaching the intersection with Lincoln Creek Trail at 4.4 miles (4,320 feet).

Walk up valley on Lincoln Creek Trail, which is moderately brushy and occasionally damp underfoot. The trail gains a gradual 320 feet in the final 3.6 miles. The campground is located near the outlet.

■ ■ ■ ■

4. MOUNT BROWN LOOKOUT

DAY HIKE
Round trip to Mount Brown Lookout: 10.6 miles (17 km)
Elevation gain: 4,300 feet (1,311 m)
High point: 7,478 feet (2,279 m)
Hiking time: 7 hours
Hikeable: mid-July through September
Difficulty: strenuous
Maps: USGS Lake McDonald East and Mount Cannon

Mount Brown Lookout is a great place to get away from the crowds and spend some time looking over the lakes, valleys, and spire-crested mountains that draw visitors to the park. This is a strenuous hike that gains 4,300 feet in 5.3 miles. Carry plenty of water, allow ample time, and start early.

Access: Drive the Going-to-the Sun Road for 11.2 miles east from its intersection with Highway 2 at the town of West Glacier. Park at Lake McDonald Lodge (elevation 3,175 feet).

The hike: Start the hike by carefully crossing the Going-to-the-Sun Road and following the Gunsight Pass–Sperry Chalet Trail through the forest. There are two junctions in the first 100 feet; stay right at both. The trail climbs, gaining nearly 1,000 feet while paralleling the deep Snyder Creek Gorge for 1.6 miles to the Mount Brown Lookout Trail intersection.

The trail to the lookout is steep, climbing to the top in twenty-nine excruciating switchbacks. (The first five switchbacks are the steepest; if you survive them, you can make it all the way.) The lookout trail breaks out into meadows created by an old

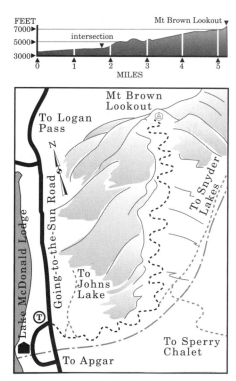

burn at switchback 24. Switchback 25 provides the first good view of the lookout, and the final switchback takes you to a high ridge top that is followed to the lookout and views.

The actual summit of 8,565-foot-high Mount Brown appears just a long hop, skip, and jump to the northeast. Beyond Mount Brown, the Little Matterhorn and a small corner of the Sperry Glacier can be seen. Hills and summits and even mountain ranges extend out in all directions. To the west Lake McDonald is visible, stretching out to the base of the Apgar Mountains.

Mount Brown Lookout

■ ■ ■ ■

5. SNYDER LAKES

DAY HIKE OR BACKPACK
Round trip to lower Snyder Lake: 8.6 miles (13.8 km)
Elevation gain: 2,035 feet (620 m)
High point: 5,210 feet (1,588 m)
Hiking time: 5 hours
Hikeable: mid-July through September
Difficulty: moderate
Maps: USGS Lake McDonald West, Lake McDonald East, and Mount
Cannon

Located in a deep cirque, surrounded by sheer cliffs and towering summits, this
small lake sits in a spectacular setting, making it easy to overlook its rather mucky
aspects. From the sheltered campsites on the lakeshore, the banded cliffs soar
up 3,000 vertical feet before touching the sky. Hunt around the talus along the
shore for rocks with ripple marks and other indications of the dramatic changes
wrought throughout the long expanse of geologic time.

Access: Drive the Going-to-the-Sun Road 11.2 miles east from its junction
with Highway 2 at West Glacier and park at Lake McDonald Lodge (3,175 feet).

The hike: Cross the Going-to-the-Sun Road and follow the Gunsight
Pass–Sperry Chalet Trail into the forest. The trail divides twice in the first 100
feet; stay right. After passing the stables on the left and the sewer plant on the
right, the wide, well-trodden trail
begins to shoot uphill. This no-
nonsense trail parallels Snyder
Creek Gorge, gaining 1,000 feet
of elevation before reaching
the Mount Brown Lookout

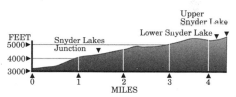

Snyder Lake

intersection at 1.6 miles. Continue straight, descending for 0.2 mile to the Snyder Lakes Trail junction at 1.8 miles.

Head off to the left on a narrow trail, which climbs steadily up Snyder Creek valley. Expect to hop across muddy sections for the entire summer. At the upper end of valley, the trail crosses an old avalanche slope covered with huckleberry bushes. When the berries are ripe, make plenty of noise between mouthfuls.

Lower Snyder Lake is reached at 4.4 miles. Campsites and an outhouse are on the right. With the massive walls of Mount Brown to the west, Edwards Mountain to the east, and the tower spires of the Little Matterhorn to the north, there are views in all directions.

No formal trail connects the lower Snyder Lake with the larger upper lake. To reach the upper lake hikers must scramble up a steep hillside and then push their way through dense brush. The best route is to follow the trail around the right side of the lower lake, cross the talus slope, then head up the left side of the creek.

■ ■ ■ ■

6. SPERRY CHALET

DAY HIKE OR BACKPACK
Round trip: 13.6 miles (21.8 km)
Elevation gain: 3,240 feet (988 m)
High point: 6,440 feet (1,963 m)
Hiking time: 2–3 days
Hikeable: August through September
Difficulty: moderate
Map: USGS Lake McDonald East

Sperry Chalet is the magnet that draws hikers to the beautiful subalpine Glacier Basin at the head of Sprague Creek. The delightful old building is an excellent place to stay, offering meals and bedding. You can even ride a horse or mule rather than walk there. The price for all this service is very steep. To avoid draining your bank account, you can purchase a backcountry permit and stay at the campsite, enjoying the scenery and resident mountain goats in peace—and with your budget intact. Although the chalet, campground, and surrounding meadows are picturesque, Glacier Basin is by no means the scenic highlight of the area. The chalet and neighboring backcountry campsite are simply a convenient, and scenic, base camp for hikes to the outstanding alpine country above.

Reservations for the chalet and nearby campground are hard to get. Make chalet reservations in January (see High Mountain Chalets in the Introduction). Camping permits are also at a premium. If you have not reserved your

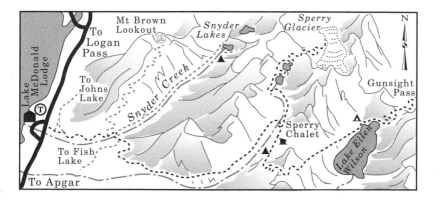

Sperry Chalet

permit ahead of time, plan to be at a backcountry reservation center by 8:00 A.M. the day before you intend to start your hike in order to reserve your site.

Access: From the West Glacier Entrance Station, drive east on the Going-to-the-Sun Road for 10.2 miles. Park at Lake McDonald Lodge (elevation 3,175 feet). The hike begins directly across the road from the parking area.

The hike: Head into the forest, following the Gunsight Pass–Sperry Chalet Trail. There are two junctions in the first 100 feet; stay to the right at both. The trail heads up the forested hillside, gaining nearly 1,000 feet in the first 1.6 miles. The climb slackens and the trail passes the Mount Brown Lookout Trail intersection (Hike 4). A few feet beyond, the Snyder Lakes Trail (Hike 5) branches off to the left. The Gunsight Pass–Sperry Chalet Trail dips to cross Snyder Creek at Crystal Ford (crossed on a wide bridge), where there is an intersection with the Fish Lake trail (Hike 1).

At 2.5 miles the trail levels and the next mile is spent traversing a forested hillside, heading for the base of the next climb. This second climb is longer and steeper than the first and considerably more interesting. After the first couple of switchbacks the monotony is broken by a view of Beaver Medicine Falls. Shortly after, the trail enters a meadow and the views expand. Before long, the chalet comes into view, perched on a rocky knoll, providing a tangible goal to those whose energies are flagging.

At 6.5 miles the trail to Sperry Glacier branches off on the left. Continue straight ahead, climbing the final 0.3 mile, to reach the chalet at 6.8 miles. Backpackers continue on with a gradual climb over the meadows for another 0.3 mile to the backcountry campsite.

Once you have set up camp, rested your legs, and cooled off your feet, it's time to head out to the high country.

Sperry Glacier: It's a 6.8-mile round-trip hike from the camp area to the glacier, with an elevation gain of 1,600 feet. The well-graded trail traverses open meadows, passes waterfalls, and wanders near three small tarns on its way to the high country. Just below 8,000-foot Comeau Pass lies a band of cliffs; the final push to the top is through a narrow cut in the rock. Steps have been created to aid the feet while a fixed rope aids the hands and the mind. The trail disappears at the pass and the route continues on over the stony ground, marked by a series of giant cairns. Remember: Do not walk on the glacier. Crevasses may be hidden under the snow and help is a long way away for those who fall in.

Gunsight Pass: The pass is an 8.8-mile round-trip hike from the backcountry campsite, and although the total elevation gain is only 500 feet, the trail manages to climb more than 1,500 feet. The entire hike is above timberline, and the views of the surrounding mountains, glaciers, meadows, and lakes make this one of the most exciting hikes in the park.

The trail leaves the camp area and climbs through flowered meadows to a 7,050-foot pass on the shoulder of Lincoln Peak, then descends to an open basin with views of Lincoln Lake and Beaver Chief Falls in an isolated valley below. After climbing a rocky

Hanging food at a backcountry campsite near Sperry Chalet

rib, the trail begins a long descent along the length of Lake Ellen Wilson, where several more backcountry campsites are located. It's a beautiful valley, but the descent is heartbreaking: After passing beneath a band of cliffs at the upper end of the lake, the trail reaches its 6,000-foot low point and the climb to 6,946-foot Gunsight Pass begins in earnest. The pass is worth the effort, with an outstanding view as your reward.

■ ■ ■ ■

7. SACRED DANCING CASCADE LOOP

DAY HIKE
Loop trip: 5 miles (8 km)
Elevation gain: 200 feet (61 m)
High point: 3,300 feet (1,006 m)
Hiking time: 3 hours
Hikeable: July through mid-October
Difficulty: easy
Map: USGS Lake McDonald East

When inclement weather keeps you out of the high country, stretch the kinks out of your legs on this scenic forest ramble to Johns Lake, Sacred Dancing Cascade, and McDonald Falls.

Access: From the West Glacier Entrance Station, drive the Going-to-the-Sun Road east for 10.2 miles to Lake McDonald Lodge (elevation 3,175 feet).

The hike: To begin the loop, walk across the Going-to-the-Sun Road and hike up the

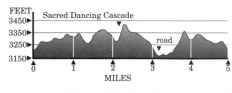

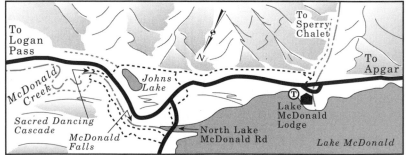

Gunsight Pass–Sperry Lake Trail for 100 feet. Pass a spur trail to the stables and, when the trail divides a second time, go left, and head up the forested valley on the Avalanche Trail. In spring and early summer the valley floor is dappled with delicate flowers; by midsummer it is awash with green from the bracken ferns, devil's club, and moss.

The trail divides several times; stay on the Avalanche Trail at all junctions. After 2 miles of walking, pass Johns Lake, a shallow pond where lilies and reeds grow in profusion. Just beyond, the trail divides again. Leave the Avalanche Trail here and take the left fork, which descends to Going-to-the-Sun Road.

The trail tunnels under the road to McDonald Creek and a bridge at the lower end of Sacred Dancing Cascade. On warm days this is a popular area for picnics. On wet days, the center of the horse bridge offers the best view of the cascade.

Once across the bridge, go left and head back down the valley along the edge of McDonald Creek for 500 feet to an intersection. There are no trail signs here,

Guided ride crossing a bridge over McDonald Creek, at the lower end of Sacred Dancing Cascade

so look for the "No Horses Allowed" sign and take the left fork. This foot trail parallels McDonald Creek for the next mile, passing McDonald Falls before ending at North Lake McDonald Road. Go left, cross McDonald Creek on the car bridge, then walk to the opposite side of the road and follow the trail along the edge of the pavement for 500 feet before heading through the trees to Going-to-the-Sun Road.

Carefully recross the Going-to-the-Sun Road, then follow the trail up the forested hillside for 500 feet to rejoin the Avalanche Trail for the final 1.5 miles back to Lake McDonald Lodge.

■ ■ ■ ■

8. TROUT AND ARROW LAKES

Trout Lake
DAY HIKE
Round trip: 7 miles (11.2 km)
Elevation gain: 2,000 feet in; 1,300 feet out (610 m in; 396 m out)
High point: 4,200 feet (1,280 m)
Hiking time: 5 hours
Hikeable: mid-June through mid-October
Difficulty: moderate
Maps: USGS Camas Ridge East and Mount Cannon

Arrow Lake
DAY HIKE OR BACKPACK
Round trip: 13.2 miles (21.1 km)
Elevation gain: 2,100 feet in; 1,300 feet out (640 m in; 396 m out)
High point: 4,200 feet (1,280 m)
Hiking time: 2 days
Hikeable: mid-June through mid-October
Difficulty: moderate
Maps: USGS Camas Ridge East and Mount Cannon

Although it is just a 3.5-mile hike into the spectacular Camas Creek valley, most park visitors overlook this quiet wilderness area with its meadows, six lakes, views, and excellent fly-fishing. There is a twofold reason for this. First, the trailhead is accessed via a narrow dirt road that is rough and full of deep potholes. Second, this is prime grizzly bear habitat.

The Lake McDonald Lodge stables offers all-day trail rides to Trout and Arrow Lakes, an alternative for those who don't like the idea of hiking a trail that is shared with bears.

Access: From the West Glacier Entrance Station, drive the Going-to-the-Sun Road east 11.7 miles to the upper end of Lake McDonald. Turn left on the North Lake McDonald Road (unsigned) and follow it for 2 miles to a small parking area and trailhead (elevation 3,230 feet).

The hike: The first 2.5 miles to Trout Lake are spent climbing steeply up a forested hillside to the 4,200-foot crest of Howe Ridge. Just before the top, the Howe Ridge Fire Trail branches off to the left. (This rarely used trail follows the forested ridge crest west. It is well marked but generally very brushy.) Continue straight, across a forested saddle, then descend

Black bear enjoying huckleberries

1,300 feet to the floor of the Camas Creek valley.

At 3.2 miles, the narrow, wet, and brushy trail to Rogers Lake and the lower Camas Creek valley branches off on the left. Passing the intersection, continue on for another 0.3 mile to Trout Lake. For day hikers the small beach alongside the trail is an ideal picnic spot and turnaround point.

Backpackers must continue on to Arrow Lake to find the backcountry campsites. The trail heads up the south side of Trout Lake, crossing avalanche slopes with stunning views of Rogers and Heavens Peaks.

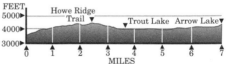

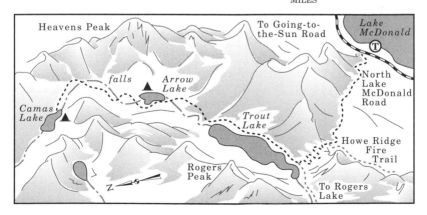

Trout Lake

At 6.6 miles the trail reaches Arrow Lake. Hikers who plan to spend several nights in the valley may continue another 3.5 miles to scenic Camas Lake, which also has a backcountry camp area.

■ ■ ■ ■

9. AVALANCHE LAKE

DAY HIKE
Round trip: 4 miles (6 km)
Elevation gain: 560 feet (171 m)
High point: 3,905 feet (1,190 m)
Hiking time: 3 hours
Hikeable: July through September
Difficulty: easy
Map: USGS Mount Cannon

Originating in the frozen mass of ice called the Sperry Glacier, rivulets of melting water come together to form creeks. These creeks descend the broad, sloping Sperry Glacier plateau, then plunge 2,000 feet down perpendicular cliffs to rest, temporarily, in the emerald waters of Avalanche Lake. Slowly the water meanders down the lake, picking up speed as it is siphoned into Avalanche Creek.

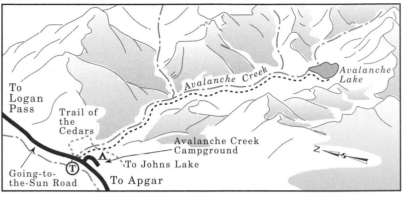

The speed increases, and in a couple of miles the waters are once again crashing and churning. The sheer force and unchained power of this stream has cut Avalanche Gorge, a deep channel through the bedrock where the water swirls and churns its way down a series of cascades. Beyond the gorge, water flows through a stately grove of western red cedars before joining McDonald Creek for a roller-coaster ride to McDonald Lake.

The journey of Avalanche Creek is a sight worth seeing, and every day during the summer hundreds of hikers make the easy trek along the creek to the shores of Avalanche Lake.

Access: From the West Glacier Entrance Station, drive the Going-to-the-Sun Road east for 15.7 miles to the Avalanche Creek Campground. Park across the

Hikers relaxing on the sandy shore of Avalanche Lake

Waterfalls cascade down the steep hillsides surrounding Avalanche Lake

road from the campground at the picnic area or, for a limited number of cars, along the road just beyond the campground.

The hike: Begin your hike with a stroll through a grove of western red cedars on the Trail of the Cedars nature loop. Near the base of Avalanche Gorge the trail divides. Head uphill to a second intersection, where you take the left fork. The trail climbs above Avalanche Gorge, then eases into a forest ramble for 2 shady miles to the lake.

You can stop as soon as you reach the lakeshore and eat your lunch on a small bench, or you can continue on to the upper end of the lake by walking the trail or the gravel beach along the lakeshore. After 0.5 mile, you are rewarded with a view of the lower portion of Monument Falls, where the foaming waters cover the rock wall in a sheet of white. The trail ends abruptly at the head of the lake. Beyond is a wall of brush, best left for the deer, bears, and other four-legged citizens of the park.

■ ■ ■ ■

10. LAKE McDONALD TRAIL

DAY HIKE OR BACKPACK
Round trip to Lake McDonald campsite: 9.2 miles (14.8 km)
Elevation gain: 150 feet (46 m)
High point: 3,200 feet (975 m)
Hiking time: 5 hours
Hikeable: mid-June through mid-October
Difficulty: easy
Map: USGS Lake McDonald West

This forested trail traverses the west shore of Lake McDonald from Fish Creek Campground to the North Lake McDonald Road. It is ideally located for guests at Fish Creek Campground who may want to stretch the kinks out of their legs after a long day of driving. It is also the perfect trail for days when the dense forest around the lakeshore is preferable to the dripping clouds and chill winds that frequently chase hikers out of the high country.

If transportation can be arranged, the trail may be hiked as a 7-mile one-way trip between the two trailheads. However, for most people, a round trip to the obvious turnaround points—Rocky Point at 0.8 mile, the lakeshore at 1.8 miles, or the backcountry campground at 4.6 miles—is preferable to the rather complicated business of arranging transportation at each end of the trail.

Access: Campers will find the trail at the northeast corner of Fish Creek Campground, near the lakeshore. Others must drive past the campground entrance, then follow the gravel-surfaced Inside North Fork Road for 0.4 mile and park in the gravel pit on the left-hand side of the road (elevation 3,280 feet).

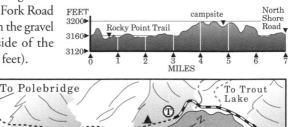

Fisherman in Lake McDonald

The hike: The trailhead is located 20 feet back down the road from the parking area, on the left. The trail descends through lodgepole forest to Fish Creek, then skirts the edge of the campground.

At 0.5 mile, a trail branches to the right, heading 0.3 mile to Rocky Point. This is a popular spot for fishermen and view seekers. It is also an excellent location to sit and watch the sunset.

The Lake McDonald trail climbs over Rocky Point and continues in dense lodgepole forest for a mile before descending to one of the few lakeshore viewpoints at 1.8 miles. The Lake McDonald backcountry campsite trail branches off on the right at 4.6 miles, providing an excellent turnaround point for day hikers.

The trail ends at 7 miles. From the trailhead it is 2.6 miles on a rough dirt road to the Lake McDonald Ranger Station and another 1.2 miles on a narrow paved road to the Going-to-the-Sun Road.

OTHER TRAILS

Fish Lake lies on the crest of Snyder Ridge on the southeast side of Lake McDonald. The forested and marshy lake is easily accessed from Sperry Chalet trail (Hike 6) and can also be reached from the Lincoln Lake trail (Hike 3).

Huckleberry Mountain Lookout is a strenuous 12-mile round trip with an elevation gain of more than 3,400 feet. The trail is accessed off the Camas Road near McGee Meadows. The mountain has a rich covering of huckleberry bushes, and bear encounters are frequent. Due to the high density of bear use, the trail is closed for much of the summer.

Golden-mantled ground squirrel

Howe Ridge, on the north side of Lake McDonald, can be traversed by a lightly maintained trail. The entire distance is in the forest. Howe Ridge Trail may be accessed from the trail to Trout and Arrow Lakes (Hike 8).

Polebridge

Polebridge is an isolated community located in the North Fork Flathead River valley on the west side of Glacier National Park. It is isolated by geography, boxed in by mountain ranges to the east and west and a closed international border to the north. It is isolated by distance; the nearest city is Columbia Falls, 41 miles to the south. It is isolated by roads that are dirt and often very rough for driving. And it is isolated by design, because the residents like it that way.

During the summer months there are three ways to drive to Polebridge. The partially paved North Fork Road may be driven all the way from Columbia Falls. From Lake McDonald the well-paved Camas Road may be driven to intersect the rough gravel of the North Fork Road at about the halfway point. The third choice is the narrow and very rough Inside North Fork Road, which starts in the Lake McDonald area at the Fish Creek Campground and stays inside the park the entire distance.

Bowman Lake

POLEBRIDGE TRAIL FINDER

Trail Number and Destination	Difficulty	Features						
		Lowland Lakes	Alpine Lakes	Waterfalls	Scenic Views	Wildlife	Fishing	Backpacking
11 Logging Lake Trail	easy	●					●	●
11 Logging Lake and Grace Lake	easy							●
12 Akokala Lake	moderate	●						●
13 Bowman Lake	easy	●					●	●
13 Brown Pass	moderate			●	●			●
14 Numa Ridge Lookout	moderate				●			
15 Quartz Lakes Loop	moderate	●					●	●
16 Kintla Lake	easy	●					●	●
16 Boulder Pass	moderate				●			●

ACCOMMODATIONS AND SERVICES

Lodging in Polebridge is limited to a few cabins near the Polebridge Mercantile and the hostel. The hostel is popular and usually booked for months in advance. It has a kitchen where guests cook their own meals, or they can dine at the small restaurant next to the Mercantile. Electricity is not available in Polebridge, so lights, stoves, and refrigerators run off kerosene or propane. Mountain bikes and some backpacking equipment may be rented at the hostel. Transportation to Polebridge can be arranged to and from the West Glacier (Belton) train station in the town of West Glacier. Write to the North Fork Hostel, Polebridge, MT 59928, or phone (406) 756-4780 for reservations and information.

The Polebridge Mercantile is an old store with a good supply of knick-knacks and some food. Regular unleaded gas is available. Inside the park, facilities include a forty-eight-site campground at Bowman Lake and a picnic area. The access road to the lake is steep, rough, and about one and one-half lanes wide. Trailers and long RVs are not allowed. The toilets are the vault type.

There is also a thirteen-site campground at Kintla Lake with a vault toilet and running water. Trailers and RVs will have a hard time on the narrow Kintla Lake Road and are not recommended.

At Big Creek, just south of the Camas Entrance Station, there is a Flathead National Forest campground. No private campgrounds or trailer facilities are available in the Polebridge area.

11. LOGGING LAKE TRAIL

Logging Lake
DAY HIKE OR BACKPACK
Round trip: 10 miles (16 km)
Elevation gain: 387 feet (118 m)
High point: 3,810 feet (1,161 m)
Hiking time: 5 hours
Hikeable: mid-June through September
Difficulty: easy
Maps: USGS Demers Ridge and Vulture Peak
Grace Lake
BACKPACK
Round trip: 25.6 miles (41 km)
Elevation gain: 577 feet (176 m)
High point: 4,000 feet (1,219 m)
Hiking time: 2–4 days
Hikeable: July through September
Difficulty: easy
Maps: USGS Demers Ridge and Vulture Peak

In an area known for its steep hills, waterfalls, and lofty summits, this hike stands out for its low elevation gain. This is a forested hike up the nearly level Logging Creek valley. For most of the trail's distance hikers meander along water, first paralleling Logging Creek, then traversing around Logging Lake. At the upper end of the lake, the trail

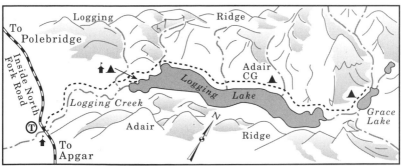

Logging Lake and Mount Geduhn

once again parallels the creek along the forested valley floor to Grace Lake.

Because of its isolated location on the west side of the park, most people plan multiday trips into this area. The trail's three camp areas generally fill to capacity throughout the summer months.

Access: The trailhead is reached by driving the narrow, rough, and winding Inside North Fork Road either 18 miles north from the Fish Creek Campground or 7.9 miles south from the Polebridge Ranger Station to Logging Creek (elevation 3,423 feet).

The hike: The trail starts out with a short climb, then levels off on a bench above Logging Creek. This is prime wildlife habitat. Deer and elk may be seen along the trail. Bears also frequent this area, so make plenty of noise, which will most likely scare away the deer and elk at the same time.

The lower end of Logging Lake is reached at 4.4 miles. The trail divides here. Straight ahead, on a pretty peninsula, lies a patrol cabin and boathouse with an excellent view up the lake to the Continental Divide. The peninsula is an ideal picnic and turnaround spot for day hikers.

Backpackers should continue up the lake. It is another 0.2 mile along the trail to the turnoff for the first campsite, located 0.3 mile to the right near the lakeshore. Adair Campground is reached at 9.4 miles from the road and, just 3.4 miles beyond, Grace Lake Campground marks the end of the official trail.

Although forested, Grace Lake is surrounded by mountains: Logging Mountain, Vulture Peak, Nahsukin Mountain, Trapper Peak, Mount Geduhn, Anaconda Peak, and Wolf Gun Mountain. To explore up valley, fishermen have beaten paths along the shore of Grace Lake, but these trails are rough and soon disappear, leaving you to continue forth as the early trappers did, crawling over logs and beating through the brush.

■ ■ ■ ■

12. AKOKALA LAKE

DAY HIKE OR BACKPACK
Round trip: 11.4 miles (18.3 km)
Elevation gain: 1,080 feet in; 540 feet out (329 m in; 165 m out)
High point: 4,840 feet (1,475 m)
Hiking time: 5 hours
Hikeable: mid-June through September
Difficulty: moderate
Maps: USGS Quartz Ridge and Kintla Peak

This pleasant ramble through the shady forest is ideal for hikers looking for a scenic destination without a great deal of climbing. Akokala Lake lies in a secluded, glacier-cut valley between Reuter Peak to the north and Numa Peak to the south. A small backcountry campsite near the lake allows you to spend a quiet evening along the lakeshore watching the fish jump.

Note: The trail is usually muddy until early August.

Access: From Apgar, drive the Camas Road 14 miles to the North Fork Road and turn right. The road is rough and

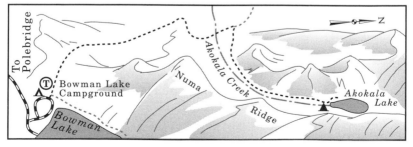

Akokala Lake

mostly gravel for the next 13.2 miles. At the Polebridge intersection, turn right and drive 1.7 miles to the Polebridge Entrance and Ranger Station. Go left on the Inside North Fork Road, drive 0.1 mile, then turn right on the rough and very narrow Bowman Lake Road. After 6 miles the road ends. Park in the backcountry hikers' area (elevation 4,030 feet).

The hike: Walk to the upper end of the campground and find the official trailhead at Site 22. The trail immediately starts a well-graded climb out of the Bowman Creek drainage. The trial climbs across a narrow toe of Numa Ridge and then descends through an open basin before reaching the trip's 4,840-foot high point.

The descent to Akokala Creek is followed by a brief climb to intersect a rarely used trail from Tepee Flat at 3.5 miles. Turn right at the junction and head up valley for the final, gradual, 2.2-mile ascent to the lake.

Passing the hitch rail is the first indication that you have reached the lake; a few steps beyond, the trail to the backcountry campsite and outhouse branches off to the right. Continue straight through the dense lodgepole forest a few more feet until the trail branches again. The right fork descends to the somewhat marshy shore. The left fork works its way through the trees and around the lake.

Take some quiet time here: this is a great place to spot moose and the occasional bear.

■ ■ ■ ■

13. BOWMAN LAKE–BROWN PASS

Bowman Lake Campground
DAY HIKE OR BACKPACK
Round trip: 13.6 miles (22 km)
Elevation gain: 100 feet (30 m)
High point: 4,030 feet (1,228 m)
Hiking time: 7 hours
Hikeable: mid-June through September
Difficulty: easy
Maps: USGS Quartz Ridge and Kintla Peak

Brown Pass
BACKPACK
Round trip: 27.6 miles (44.2 km)
Elevation gain: 2,225 feet (678 m)
High point: 6,255 feet (1,906 m)
Hiking time: 2–3 days
Hikeable: mid-July through mid-September
Difficulty: moderate
Maps: USGS Quartz Ridge, Kintla Peak, and Mt. Carter

Fjordlike Bowman Lake is a narrow, 7-mile-long finger of water boxed in by steep mountains. This is a beautiful setting for a family stroll, an easy backpack, or an extended journey up the Bowman Creek valley to the Continental Divide and the alpine meadows at Brown Pass.

Canoeing Bowman Lake

If you are planning an overnight trip, it is best to obtain your permits at the Apgar Visitor Center before heading north to Polebridge. Permits are also issued at the Polebridge Ranger Station, but only when someone is available to do it.

Access: From Apgar, drive north on Camas Road 14 miles to the North Fork Road and turn right. The road is rough and mostly gravel for the next 13.2 miles. At the Polebridge intersection, turn right and drive 1.7 miles to the Polebridge Entrance and Ranger Station. Go left on the Inside North Fork Road, drive 0.1 mile, then turn right on the rough and very narrow Bowman Lake Road. After 6 miles the road ends. Park in the backcountry hikers' area (elevation 4,030 feet).

The hike: The trail begins at the boat launching area and heads north, around the end of the lake. Pass the ranger's residence, then head into the forest. At 0.7 mile a trail branches left to Numa Ridge Lookout (Hike 14). Stay right.

As you head up Bowman Lake, Rainbow Peak, Mount Carter, and Thunderbird Mountain come into view to the southeast. Near the head of the lake, at 6.8 miles, you pass a backcountry camp area. This is the turnaround point for day hikers and an overnight stop for backpackers.

Beyond the lake, the trail

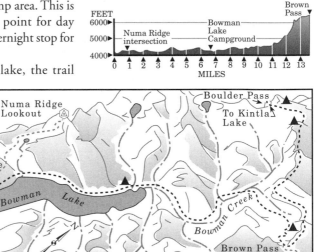

Bowman Lake

heads through forest, up the swampy Bowman Creek valley for 3 miles before beginning a long climb across the lower flanks of Chapman Peak. Near the top, the trail leaves the forest, providing views to the west.

A waterfall marks the entrance to the basin just below the pass. Shortly beyond, at 13.5 miles from the trailhead, is the Brown Pass backcountry campsite. Then it's 0.3 mile of relatively easy walking to 6,255-foot Brown Pass, where the Bowman Lake Trail meets the Boulder Pass Trail and ends. Take advantage of any spare time to do some high-country exploring of the exquisite alpine meadows at Hole-in-the-Wall and Boulder Pass. If a shuttle car is available, try the excellent hike from Brown Pass to Kintla Lake (Hike 16).

■ ■ ■ ■

14. NUMA RIDGE LOOKOUT

DAY HIKE
Round trip: 11.4 miles (18 km)
Elevation gain: 2,930 feet (1,523 m)
High point: 6,960 feet (2,744 m)
Hiking time: 6 hours
Hikeable: mid-July through September
Difficulty: moderate
Maps: USGS Quartz Ridge and Kintla Peak

A view that encompasses the magnificent grandeur of the glacier-carved Bowman Valley; the jade-colored waters of Bowman Lake; the massive Rainbow, Square, and Carter Mountains to the east; and the broad North Fork Flathead River valley and forested Whitefish Range to the west is the reward for the long climb to the Numa Ridge Lookout.

The trail to this magnificent view is well graded, allowing for a gradual climb from the shores of the lake to the lookout. Be sure to carry plenty of water; the ridge is dry.

Access: From Apgar, drive north on Camas Road 14 miles to the North Fork Road and turn right. The road is rough and mostly gravel for the next 13.2 miles. At the Polebridge intersection, turn right and drive 1.7 miles to the Polebridge Entrance and Ranger Station. Go left on the Inside North Fork Road, drive 0.1 mile, then turn right on the rough and very narrow Bowman Lake Road. After 6 miles the road ends. Park in the backcountry hikers' area (elevation 4,030 feet).

The hike: Follow the Bowman Lake Trail from the boat

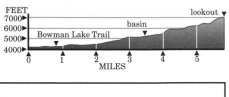

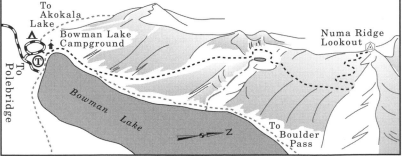

launch area, past the ranger station, and along the northwest shore of the lake for 0.7 mile to a junction. Go left on the Numa Ridge Trail and head uphill. The climb is gradual, with an elevation gain of only 1,000 feet in the next 2.8 miles.

At 3.5 miles there is a short descent into a wooded basin (5,120 feet) where a small, nameless pond is hidden in the trees on the right. The trail then begins to climb with a bit more determination, heading to the open meadows and views. Before long, you will see both Bowman Lake and forested Cerulean Ridge. To the west, north, and south are the minor and major summits of the Whitefish Range.

The lookout is located on a 6,960-foot crest of a minor bump on Numa Ridge. The building is occupied during times of high fire danger at the end of the summer. Hikers may walk up the stairs and wander around the balcony, which is a great place to scan the open hillsides for wildlife. In late summer, look for bears grazing on the huckleberries in the basin below.

Hiker near the crest of Numa Ridge

■ ■ ■ ■

15. QUARTZ LAKES LOOP

DAY HIKE OR BACKPACK
Loop trip: 12.8 miles (20.5 km)
Elevation gain: 2,279 feet (695 m)
High point: 5,400 feet (1,646 m)
Hiking time: 7 hours
Hikeable: mid-June through September
Difficulty: moderate
Map: USGS Quartz Ridge

Here is where you will find three lakes with the same name on one loop trail with the same name. The three Quartz Lakes are surrounded by forest, perfect destinations for high-country hikers when the weather is poor or for fishermen looking for cutthroat in any weather. Serious fishermen can make a good catch from the lakeshore; those who need to nudge Lady Luck a little should add a small raft or belly float to their packs.

The two backcountry campgrounds make excellent overnight stops for those who do not choose to race around the loop in a single day. The lakeside camp area at Quartz Lake is recommended for the view you will have from your tent door; however, no fires are allowed. Campsites at Lower Quartz Lake are sheltered in the trees and fires are permitted.

If you plan to overnight on the trail, obtain your permit from the

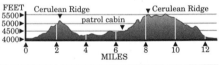

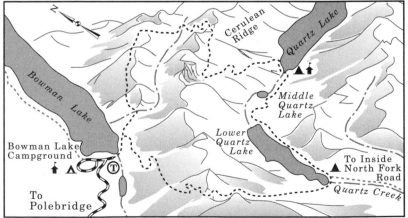

Caption goes here

Backpackers crossing a log bridge over Quartz Creek

Apgar Visitor Center before heading north.

Access: From Apgar, drive the Camas Road 14 miles to the North Fork Road and turn right. The road is rough and mostly gravel for the next 13.2 miles. At the Polebridge intersection, turn right and drive 1.7 miles to the Polebridge Entrance and Ranger Station. Go left on the Inside North Fork Road, drive 0.1 mile, then turn right on the rough and very narrow Bowman Lake Road. After 6 miles the road ends. Park in the backcountry hikers' area (4,030 feet).

The hike: Walk to the shore of Bowman Lake, then turn right and head south on a trail that crosses the outlet on a footbridge, then passes a ranger residence. At 0.4 mile the trail leaves the lakeshore and divides, marking the start of the loop.

This trip description begins with the right fork so that the steep portion of the trail can be climbed early in the day. Backpackers may prefer the meandering style of the left fork, which allows for a gradual climb over Cerulean Ridge.

Heading right, the trail climbs 1,070 feet over 5,100-foot Cerulean Ridge, then drops to Lower Quartz Lake in just 3.1 miles. The climb is steep and rough and never bothers with any unnecessary rambling. At the top of the ridge, take time to enjoy the view over the Quartz Creek

Patrol cabin at Quartz Lake

valley before descending straight down through the burn of 1988 to Lower Quartz Lake (4,191 feet).

On the east side of Quartz Creek, in the middle of the camp cooking area, the trail divides. The right fork is a rarely used trail that descends 6.9 miles to the Inside North Fork Road. The left fork is the loop trail that heads up the valley, and at 6 miles 4,397-foot Middle Quartz Lake comes into view. Shortly beyond, the trail recrosses Quartz Creek, then climbs a small rise and descends to Quartz Lake. The trail passes a patrol cabin before it reaches the camp area at 6.6 miles (4,416 feet).

Leaving Quartz Lake, the loop route heads back up to the crest of Cerulean Ridge. Once on top, the trail begins to wander, making a complete tour of the forested hillside before descending back to Bowman Lake.

■ ■ ■ ■

16. KINTLA LAKE AND THE BOULDER PASS TRAIL

Kintla Lake camp
DAY HIKE OR BACKPACK
Round trip: 12.6 miles (21 km)
Elevation gain: 160 feet (49 m)
High point: 4,160 feet (1,268 m)
Hiking time: 6 hours
Hikeable: mid-June through September
Difficulty: easy
Map: USGS Kintla Lake

Boulder Pass
BACKPACK
Round trip: 35.4 miles (57 km)
Elevation gain: 3,462 feet (1,055 m)
High point: 7,470 feet (2,277 m)
Hiking time: 3–4 days
Hikeable: August through mid-September
Difficulty: moderate
Maps: USGS Kintla Lake, Kintla Peak, Mt. Carter, and Porcupine Ridge

Boulder Pass is one of the favorite backcountry areas of Glacier National Park hikers. It is hard to describe the area without tripping over an endless string of superlatives, so let it suffice to say that the meadows and rocky summits make the long hike worthwhile.

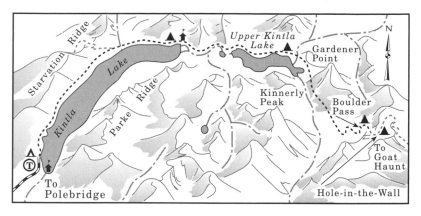

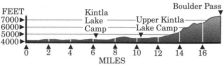

The ideal way to hike the Boulder Pass Trail is to follow it all the way from Kintla Lake to Goat Haunt at the upper end of Waterton Lake. However, for most people, even those with two vehicles at their disposal, the transportation logistics are too difficult and time-consuming. Most

Hiker near the backcountry campsite at the upper end of Kintla Lake

hikers find it easier to establish a base camp at Boulder Pass and spend a day or more exploring.

Access: Arrange your backcountry permits at the Apgar Visitor Center, then drive to Polebridge. Once in the park, turn left on the Inside North Fork Road and drive 14.7 miles to road's end at Kintla Lake. The road is narrow and some sections are rough, so allow plenty of time for the drive. Day hikers park in a special area near the lake; backpackers must leave their cars at the overnight parking area at the west side of the campground (elevation 4,015 feet).

The hike: Unlike many of the other popular trails in the park, this one has retained its rustic feel with roots and rocks in the narrow track. The result is a trail with a real wilderness flavor.

At the upper end of Kintla Lake, 6.3 miles from the start, the trail passes through a backcountry camp area, scenically located near the lakeshore, with views of Kinnerly Peak and Boundary Mountain. Just 0.2 mile beyond, a patrol cabin at the end of the lake marks the start of a 2.5-mile forest walk to Upper Kintla Lake.

Kintla Lake

The trail skirts around Upper Kintla Lake for 2 miles and passes a backcountry campsite near the upper end. Beyond the lake, it's time to grit your teeth for the 5-mile climb to the pass. The trail is steep and very warm in the afternoon heat. At 5,200 feet the switchbacks begin, and the climb is relentless until the trail reaches a high bench at 7,200 feet. When the climb tapers off, the trail heads through a beautiful larch forest, which is replaced by open meadows at the pass.

The Boulder Pass camp area is located 17.2 miles from the start; just 0.5 mile beyond is 7,470-foot Boulder Pass. If you have a good map and compass, explore the small tarns below Gardener Point, look for the colorful boulder fields on the ridge crest above the pass, or stroll down to Hole-in-the-Wall.

■ ■ ■ ■

OTHER TRAILS

Quartz Creek Trail runs from Quartz Creek Campground to Lower Quartz Lake (Hike 15). This trail sees moderate use, mostly from horse parties.

Other trails, such as **Kishenehn Creek**, **Akokala Creek,** and **Dutch Creek,** receive at most an annual clearing of fallen logs and are used primarily for fire fighting.

Walton

Walton lies at the often-ignored or just-plain-forgotten southern corner of Glacier National Park, near the small community of Essex. Civilization's main encroachments in this narrow section of the Middle Fork Flathead River valley are Highway 2 and the railroad tracks. On the north side of the valley, the pristine wilderness of Glacier National Park begins a few feet from the road; to the south, the Great Bear and Bob Marshall Wilderness Areas preserve a huge tract of the Rocky Mountains along the crest of the Continental Divide.

Little Dog Mountain from the summit of Elk Mountain

WALTON TRAIL FINDER

Trail Number and Destination	Difficulty	Features						
		Lowland Lakes	Alpine Lakes	Waterfalls	Scenic Views	Wildlife	Fishing	Backpacking
17 Goat Lick	easy					●		
18 Nyack–Coal Creek Wilderness Camping Zone	difficult		●	●		●		●
19 Scalplock Mountain Lookout	strenuous				●			
20 Elk Mountain	strenuous				●			
Isabel Lake	strenuous						●	
Harrison Lake	strenuous	●						●
Loneman Lookout	strenuous				●			
Park Creek	strenuous							●
Ole Creek	strenuous							●

ACCOMMODATIONS AND SERVICES

The only service offered by the park at Walton is a small picnic area located next to the ranger station. It has picnic tables and pit toilets. No park lodging, camping, or even water are available here.

The nearest overnight accommodations are found at the Izaak Walton Inn in Essex. The railroad-themed inn is located next to the railroad tracks. Guests may stay in the inn or in remodeled cabooses. Other motels are located a few miles to the west on Highway 2. Private campgrounds are located to the east and west of Walton; Forest Service campgrounds can be found to the east along Highway 2.

■ ■ ■ ■

17. WALTON AREA SHORT HIKES

Ole Creek. This short, easy 1-mile round-trip hike to Ole Creek and the delta at its confluence with the Middle Fork Flathead River is an easy stroll along the ancient terraces above the river. The trail begins at the Walton Picnic Area and wanders through the forest to the creek. Walk across the suspension bridge, then leave the main trail and follow an unmarked path to the river.

Goat Lick. The Goat Lick is the most popular attraction in the Walton area. Located on the south side of Highway 2 just 1.7 miles east of the Walton Ranger Station, it is a unique area where the mountain goats come down from the ridge tops to lick mineral salt deposits. At the lick or on the slopes above it as many as fifty animals have been seen at one time. Elk and deer also make occasional visits. The best time for view-

Viewing platform at Goat Lick

ing is in June and July, during the early mornings or late afternoons. The best views are reached by a very short and easy walk from the parking lot.

Scientists are not sure why goats and other wildlife crave salt. It may have something to do with the change of diet in the spring, or it may be simply an acquired taste (like sugar is for humans).

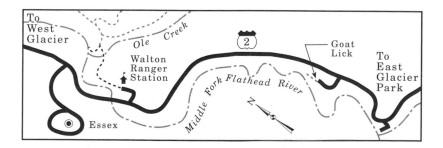

■ ■ ■ ■

18. NYACK–COAL CREEK WILDERNESS CAMPING ZONE

BACKPACK
Loop trip: 39.9 miles (63.8 km)
Elevation gain: 2,590 feet (789 m)
High point: 6,090 feet (1,856 m)
Hiking time: 4–6 days
Hikeable: August through September
Difficulty: difficult
Maps: USGS Nyack, Stanton Lake, Mt. Jackson, Mt. Stimson, and
Mt. St. Nicholas

If you are coming to Glacier National Park seeking solitude and true wilderness, this is the hike for you. Most of the trip is through forested valley bottoms with none of the high mountain vistas that draw hikers by the thousands to other areas of the park. The trails are rough: fallen trees may lie for months before they are cleared, brush may obscure the path, and bridges, for the most part, are nonexistent. A good set of maps is required as trails may be obscured in the brush and may completely disappear in the meadows.

On the positive side of the ledger, although there are designated campsites, you don't have to stay in them. You can do this hike on your own schedule without worrying about where your permit says you have to be each night. It is a wonderful way to experience the true wilderness. Crowds are never a problem and exploration is the order of the day, offering an unprecedented opportunity to see the park in a nearly natural state.

To start the hike, you must ford the Middle Fork Flathead River. Hikers and horses alike will have trouble with the crossing in early summer. Hikers

Hiker fording the deep waters of Middle Fork Flathead River in September

should wait until at least late August before attempting the crossing.

Although hikers are not required to pitch their tents in designated camp areas, there are four sites on the loop where you can stay if you would like to have a campfire or if you are traveling with stock. Hikers who choose to overnight away from the designated areas must carry a stove and use low-impact techniques. It is also extremely important to follow all the rules pertaining to hiking and camping in bear country, such as hanging food and cooking well away from the sleeping area.

Note: Backcountry permits are required, even if you are not camping in a designated area. When picking up a backcountry permit, also obtain a copy of the Nyack trailhead map, which shows the ford area in detail.

Access: Drive Highway 2 east for 10.9 miles from the town of West Glacier. Turn left on a gravel road and head north 0.2 mile to a T intersection. Go right, pass a hitching rail, and park off the road in the meadow (elevation 3,351 feet).

The hike: Walk the old road along the edge of the railroad tracks. When the road ends, cross the tracks and find an obscure trail on the opposite side that heads through the cottonwoods to the river. Walk across the gravel bar to the river's edge. Looking across, find the place on the opposite shore where the gravel bar meets a grassy bank. Head straight across at this point. On the north side, the trail crosses a grassy area and an old river channel before reaching the official trail sign.

Just beyond the site of the old Nyack Ranger Station, intersect the South Boundary Trail and go left, downstream,

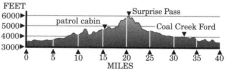

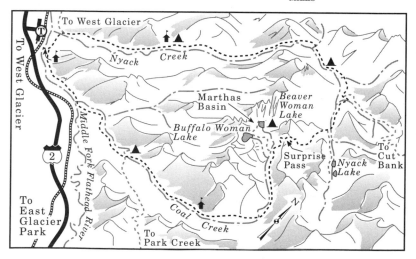

for 0.7 mile to the Nyack Creek Trail, then turn right and head up the Nyack Creek valley. At 7.2 miles from the Middle Fork ford, the trail passes a patrol cabin. The valley bottom narrows, then widens, and the views improve as the trail heads into the mountains. A second patrol cabin is passed at 15.3 miles. At 16.9 miles, the trail to Cut Bank and Pitamakan Passes heads off to the east. Leave the Nyack Creek Trail at 19.1 miles (4,800 feet) and begin to climb on the Surprise Pass Trail.

It takes 2.5 miles of steady climbing to reach 5,900-foot Surprise Pass. The trail then descends to meet the Coal Creek Trail, 21.6 miles from the Middle Fork. The loop route heads left, down Coal Creek. The right fork heads up to Beaver Woman and Buffalo Woman Lakes at 6,090 feet, in Marthas Basin, well worth the 1.4-mile side trip.

The Coal Creek Trail descends, passing an intersection with the Fielding Creek Trail at 30.4 miles from the Middle Fork and ending at the South Boundary Trail at 36.1 miles. Head west for a final 3.8 miles to complete the loop at the old Nyack Ranger Station.

Hiker on the Nyack Creek Trail

■ ■ ■ ■

19. SCALPLOCK MOUNTAIN LOOKOUT

DAY HIKE
Round trip: 9 miles (14.4 km)
Elevation gain: 3,199 feet (975 m)
High point: 6,919 feet (2,109 m)
Hiking time: 6 hours
Hikeable: mid-July through September
Difficulty: strenuous
Map: USGS Essex

Fire lookouts are generally an indication that there will be panoramic views. Scalplock Mountain is no exception. Hikers can find superb vistas from the balcony of the lookout. (The tower is staffed in times of extreme fire danger.) First-time visitors to the summit should carry a detailed map to help identify mountains and valleys that radiate out from Scalplock Mountain like spokes from a wheel. Luckily, this trail is off the beaten path—otherwise one would expect park visitors to flock to this expansive viewpoint.

Access: From the town of West Glacier, drive Highway 2 east for 26.5 miles. Cross the Middle Fork Flathead River bridge, then turn left to the Walton Ranger Station and picnic area. Leave your car in the small backcountry parking area (elevation 3,720 feet). Be sure to carry an ample supply of water; the climb to the summit is long, steep, and very dry.

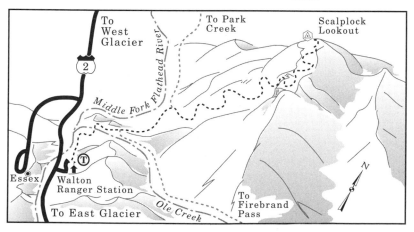

Hikers on the balcony of Scalplock Mountain Lookout

The hike: From the picnic area, the trail heads down the forested valley for 0.4 mile to Ole Creek. Once across the very springy suspension bridge, the trail begins to climb.

The trail levels off shortly before reaching the first intersection at 1 mile. Take the left fork. At 1.3 miles the trail divides for the second and last time. Go right and begin the climb up Scalplock on the first of many switchbacks.

Most of the hike is in the forest; however, occasional openings provide fascinating views of the Middle Fork Flathead River valley, the community of Essex, and the Flathead Range. As you continue up the steep hillside, watch the trains come and go through the Essex switching yard, adding engines for the climb over Marias Pass or unhooking them in preparation for the next eastbound train.

An open ridge is reached at 3.7 miles, and for the first time on this hike the views extend to the east over the Ole Creek valley, into the heart of the park. The trail ends at 4.5 miles, on the crest of the 6,919-foot summit of Scalplock Mountain.

At the summit, spread out the map and locate the places you have visited and the places you would like to hike to before you leave the park. Don't ignore the Flathead Range to the southwest. It is easy to see that there is plenty of beautiful country to explore beyond the borders of the park.

WEATHER

As in any mountainous environment, the weather in Glacier and Waterton Lakes National Parks is predictably unpredictable. In general, the climate on the west side of the mountains is wetter than the east side, so it is possible for it to be raining at Lake McDonald and sunny at St. Mary. The east side valleys see more afternoon thunder and lightning storms than the west side.

The east side of Glacier National Park and all of Waterton Lakes National Park are windier than the west side. Situated in the middle, Logan Pass has its own microclimate, which can be better or worse than the lowland valleys.

In the summer, daytime conditions may exceed 90 degrees and temperatures may drop to near freezing at night.

The following chart gives a guide to average park conditions. However, in order to get the most out of your visit, always plan for the extremes. Remember that snowfall during the summer at Logan Pass is not uncommon.

PRECIPITATION AND TEMPERATURE CHART

	PRECIPITATION		TEMPERATURE	
	Average (inches)	Average number of days with precipitation	Average maximum temperature	Average minimum temperature
January	3.40	17	28	15
February	2.37	13	35	19
March	1.86	13	42	23
April	1.81	11	53	30
May	2.57	13	64	27
June	3.28	13	71	44
July	1.75	9	79	47
August	1.64	9	78	46
September	2.06	9	67	39
October	2.33	11	53	32
November	3.10	15	37	25
December	3.30	17	30	18

■ ■ ■ ■

20. ELK MOUNTAIN

DAY HIKE
Round trip: 7.5 miles (13 km)
Elevation gain: 3,355 feet (1,023 m)
High point: 7,835 feet (2,388 m)
Hiking time: 6 hours
Hikeable: mid-July through September
Difficulty: strenuous
Map: USGS Walton

If you love the wonderful national park scenery but wish you could enjoy the views without the crowds, Elk Mountain may be just what you are looking for.

Elk Mountain was once the site of a fire lookout and the view from the summit is extensive: it includes the rugged summits of the Great Bear and Bob Marshall Wildernesses as well as some of the wildest areas of Glacier National Park.

Despite the impressive view, the trail is rarely traveled. This isolation is due, in part, to the odd access on private land and the unmarked parking. However, the main impediment is the extremely steep trail that climbs 3,000 feet in just 3 miles.

Carry plenty of water and get an early start to avoid the heat.

Access: On Highway 2, drive east 10.6 miles from Walton Ranger Station or 17 miles west of the town of East Glacier. At milepost 192, turn northwest on an unmarked dirt road. Pass a gravel pit and at 0.4 mile from the highway find a place to park in one of the wide spots on the right side of the road (elevation 4,480 feet).

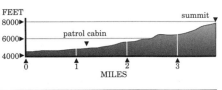

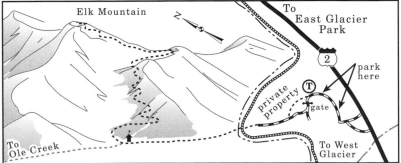

Trail approaching the summit of Elk Mountain

The hike: Walk up the road a short 0.1 mile to find the Fielding–Coal Creek Trail access sign on the right. Follow the narrow trail up the short hill where it joins an old road. Continue to ascend through a large clearcut for a mile to the railroad tracks.

Once across the double tracks go left until you find the well-marked Fielding–Coal Creek Trail and the national park boundary. For the next 0.2 mile follow the trail through a thick grove of lodgepole pines. At 1.3 miles from the car, the trail enters a clearing and passes a well-maintained patrol cabin. At the far end of the clearing find an intersection. Go right on the narrow and rarely traveled Elk Mountain Trail.

Initially the trail meanders along the base of the mountain. Enjoy the easy part; all too soon the trail transforms into a no-nonsense race to the summit. With no frivolous switchbacks or meandering traverses, the trail rockets up the hillside with views expanding with each twist and turn. An open ridge crest at 7,200 feet provides a brief respite before the final push to the summit.

Hikers enjoying the view from the summit of Elk Mountain

The 7,855-foot summit is worth the effort. The view is magnificent. Below your feet lies the deep Ole Creek valley, and beyond is Grizzly Peak, Chief Lodgepole Peak, and Mount Rockwell.

■ ■ ■ ■

OTHER TRAILS

Harrison Lake lies on the southern side of the park and is rarely visited. When the water is low—in late August and September—hikers can ford the Middle Fork Flathead River for an easy 3-mile hike to the lake. Visitors in early season must start at the West Glacier Entrance Station for a 10-mile stroll up the moderately maintained South Boundary Trail to the Harrison Lake turnoff. (If you plan to ford the river, check in at Apgar Visitor Center and pick up a map.)

Loneman Lookout is a strenuous hike to a rewarding viewpoint. The shortest access is to ford the Middle Fork Flathead River (safe only in late August through September). The trail gains nearly 4,000 feet in the 6.5 miles from the ford to the summit. The alternative access is to hike the South Boundary Trail east 12 miles from the town of West Glacier, followed by a 5.2-mile climb to the summit.

Park Creek Trail is an invitation to solitude. This 17-mile-long trail starts at the Walton Ranger Station and ends at the shores of Lake Isabel at the base of Battlement Mountain. Lake Isabel may also be reached from the Two Medicine area via the scenic Cobalt Lake Trail.

Ole Creek Trail is a 15.5-mile trudge up a forested valley to Ole Lake. The trail continues over Firebrand Pass and out to Highway 2 (Hike 27).

Autumn Creek Trail is part of the Continental Divide Trail in the summer and a popular cross-country touring area in the winter. The trail is easily accessed from Marias Pass summit on Highway 2. In East Glacier, find the trailhead behind (west of) the Glacier Park Lodge at the Midvale Creek Bridge.

Two Medicine and East Glacier Park

The Two Medicine area is one of the most scenic regions of the park. Visitors can easily access breathtaking viewpoints, lakes, waterfalls, and incredible high alpine vistas. Visitors also have a wide choice of short hikes, comfortable day hikes, and extended backpack trips.

It is worth noting that Two Medicine is the only major park access that does not have a lodge. Accommodations for this area are located outside the park boundary in the town of East Glacier Park.

TWO MEDICINE AND EAST GLACIER PARK TRAIL FINDER

Trail Number and Destination	Difficulty	Features						
		Lowland Lakes	Alpine Lakes	Waterfalls	Scenic Views	Wildlife	Fishing	Backpacking
21 Running Eagle Falls	easy			●				
21 Paradise Point	easy	●					●	
21 Aster Falls	easy			●				
21 Twin Falls	easy			●				
22 Scenic Point	moderate				●			
23 Two Medicine Lake Circuit	easy	●						
24 Cobalt Lake	moderate		●	●	●			●
25 Upper Two Medicine Lake	easy	●		●				●
26 Dawson Pass Loop	strenuous	●	●	●	●	●	●	●
27 Firebrand Pass	moderate				●	●		

Hiker near Dawson Pass on the Dawson Pass Loop

ACCOMMODATIONS AND SERVICES

The most important feature of East Glacier Park is the Amtrak station. Visitors arriving by train can arrange for a rental car to be waiting at the station, or they can be picked up by a vintage Red Bus and whisked across the street to the Glacier Park Lodge.

If the lodge is not in your price range, try one of several motels or the youth hostel (Brownies Grocery and Hostel). Food is not a problem either, with several restaurants, fast-food outlets, and a small general store to choose from. The lodge offers such amenities as a golf course and several lowland hikes.

Two Medicine has a large campground, including a hiker/biker area with food storage boxes for campers without vehicles. The campground is often full by noon during the busy summer season. If you arrive late in the day, try the Red Eagle Campground, a private facility, located at the Highway 49 turnoff.

Backcountry permits and general information can be obtained from the small ranger station at the campground entrance. It is open daily from 8:00 A.M. to 5:00 P.M. from mid-June to Labor Day.

The small general store located at Two Medicine Lake sells some groceries, camping supplies, and a lot of souvenirs. There is also a snack bar that sells hot coffee and sandwiches.

The *Sinopah*, a small tour boat, makes four trips a day up the 2-mile-long Two Medicine Lake. If you take the first cruise in the morning, you can spend the day hiking from the upper end of the lake to destinations such as Upper Two Medicine Lake, No Name Lake, or Dawson Pass, then ride the last boat down the lake in the afternoon.

Rowboats, canoes, and boats with small electric motors are available to rent when the wind is not howling.

21. TWO MEDICINE AREA SHORT HIKES

Running Eagle Falls. An easy 0.6-mile round trip, with no elevation gain, leads to a falls where the water shoots out of the rocky hillside. The trail begins 1.2 miles past the Two Medicine Entrance Station. A portion of the trail is wheelchair accessible.

Paradise Point. This is an easy 1.2-mile round-trip stroll, with only 100 feet of elevation gain, to a scenic peninsula on Two Medicine Lake. The trail begins from the end of the Two Medicine Road. Walk past the boathouse and follow the South Shore Trail through forest, then meadows, for 0.2 mile to an intersection. Turn right and walk another 0.4 mile to a gravel beach at the end of the point.

Aster Falls. The destination of this 2.4-mile round-trip walk, with a 100-foot elevation gain, is a pretty waterfall. The trail begins from the end of the Two Medicine Road. Walk past the boathouse, then follow the South Shore Trail. After a meandering 1.1 miles, go left. After 0.1 mile the trail divides again; go left again to the falls.

Twin Falls. From the boat dock at

South Shore Trail near Aster Falls

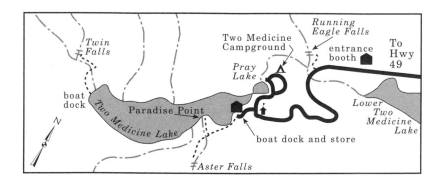

Running Eagle Falls

the upper end of Two Medicine Lake, the falls is an easy 1.8-mile round trip with no elevation gain. The wide, well-signed trail to the falls passes through forest and flower-covered meadows.

■ ■ ■ ■

22. SCENIC POINT

DAY HIKE
Round trip: 6.2 miles (9.9 km)
Elevation gain: 2,262 feet (689 m)
High point: 7,522 feet (2,292 m)
Hiking time: 4 hours
Hikeable: July through September
Difficulty: moderate
Map: USGS Squaw Mountain

Scenic Point is a misnomer; it's not just one point that is scenic, it's an entire mountain with outstanding views that extend over the Two Medicine area and beyond into the wilderness section of Glacier National Park.

The trail to Scenic Point is well graded with a continuous climb. Some sections of trail were blasted out of solid rock; other sections were etched across the loose talus slopes. To best enjoy this hike, wear sturdy shoes and carry plenty of water for the ascent over the open hillsides.

Access: From the Two Medicine Entrance Station, drive Two Medicine Road 3.3 miles up the valley. The trailhead is located on the left as the road begins its descent toward Two Medicine Lake. From the opposite direction, the trailhead is located 0.2 mile above the Two Medicine Campground entrance.

The hike: The trail begins near the entrance of the parking area (elevation 5,260 feet) and heads into the forest, climbing gradually. At 0.5 mile a side trail branches off on the right to the Appistoki Falls viewpoint.

Beyond the falls intersection, the trail begins to climb in earnest. It takes seventeen switchbacks to reach the top of Scenic Point. However, there is no need to wait for switchback seventeen before you start picking out landmarks. The views begin at the second switchback, where you can look up the Appistoki Creek basin to Mount Henry and Appistoki Peak. To the north, Spot Mountain, Two Medicine Ridge, and the Day Fork Creek valley come into view. By the fifteenth switchback, all of Two Medicine Lake can be seen, as well as Rising Wolf Mountain, Bighorn Basin, Dawson Pass, Pumpelly Pillar, Upper Two Medicine Lake, and a portion of Lower Two Medicine Lake.

At the seventeenth switchback, the trail crosses a narrow saddle with an excellent view. It is a good-enough destination for anyone who might not feel comfortable with exposure. To continue on, head up the ridge 100 feet or so, then go left on a narrow trail that traverses a precipitous slope that should not be attempted if there is snow. Once across, the trail traverses a rocky

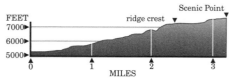

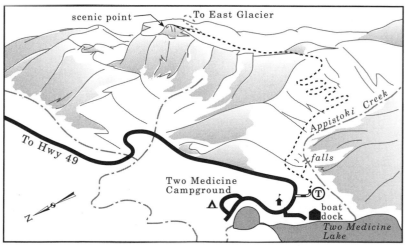

plateau. A sign at the far end marks the point where you head left, uphill, to the actual summit of Scenic Point. There is no trail here, so stay on rocks as much as possible while crossing the fragile vegetation on the open hillside.

At the 7,522-foot summit of Scenic Point, views expand to encompass the eastern plains of Montana. Below your feet are the towns of East Glacier Park and Browning, and beyond you can almost see Cut Bank, Shelby, Fargo, and New York.

The trail continues on, dropping down into the forest, to end at the outskirts of East Glacier Park.

Weathered tree and Two Medicine valley from the Scenic Point trail

■ ■ ■ ■

23. TWO MEDICINE LAKE CIRCUIT

DAY HIKE
Loop trip: 7.2 miles (11.5 km)
Elevation gain: 276 feet (84 m)
High point: 5,440 feet (1,658 m)
Hiking time: 4 hours
Hikeable: July through mid-October
Difficulty: easy
Maps: USGS Squaw Mountain and Mt. Rockwell

Pack the binoculars and a substantial lunch for this hike around Two Medicine Lake. The binoculars will come in handy for spotting bighorn sheep, mountain goats, bears, and birds on the lake and on the open slopes above. The lunch needs no explanation.

The basic loop around the lake is 7.2 miles. However, you can easily add a mile or two by exploring the side trails that lead to waterfalls, other lakes, or a vista point.

Access: From the Two Medicine Entrance, drive Two Medicine Road to its end. Park near the store (elevation 5,164 feet).

The hike: Walk past the boathouse and enter the forest, following the South Shore Trail. At 0.2 mile is an intersection and your first opportunity to stray from the basic circuit. On the right, a trail heads 0.4 mile out to the tip of Paradise Point, where you can sit on a gravel beach and enjoy a sweeping view of the lake.

The South Shore Trail ducks in and out of the trees for the next 0.5 mile. Shortly after you

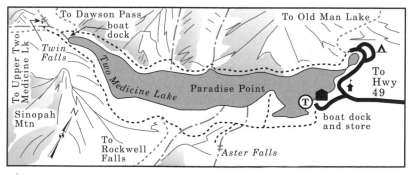

The view east, down Two Medicine Lake

cross Aster Creek, a trail branches off on the left, designed to lure hikers off the circuit route for a 0.1-mile side trip to the base of Aster Falls.

Continue through the forest to Paradise Creek, which is crossed on a bouncy, swaying suspension bridge that is removed in the winter. At 2.4 miles, the trail to Rockwell Falls and Cobalt Lake branches off to the left. The falls, located just 1.1 nearly level miles up this trail, is another popular side trip.

Beyond the intersection, the lake trail climbs to its 5,440-foot high point on a brushy slope of Sinopah Mountain where there are views of the lake, Pumpelly Pillar, and Rising Wolf Mountain.

By 3.4 miles you have passed the upper end of the lake and returned to the valley floor. At the intersection with the Upper Boat Dock Trail, go left and walk up valley for a level 0.5 mile to Two Medicine Creek and another intersection. To the left, Twin Falls is a short 0.3-mile side trip, and Upper Medicine Lake is a slightly longer but easy 1.7-mile trip.

The circuit route goes to the right, starting back down the lake. At 4.1 miles is an intersection with the Dawson Pass Trail. Turn right and walk through a cool forest with occasional glimpses of the lake. The trail passes around Pray Lake before ending in the campground. Walk to the right, through the campground, to finish the loop back to the store.

■ ■ ■ ■

24. COBALT LAKE

DAY HIKE OR BACKPACK
Round trip: 11.4 miles (18.2 km)
Elevation gain: 1,406 feet (429 m)
High point: 6,570 feet (2,002 m)
Hiking time: 6 hours
Hikeable: mid-July through September
Difficulty: moderate
Maps: USGS Squaw Mountain and Mt. Rockwell

The colorful setting makes this lake stand out from all the other beautiful lakes in Glacier National Park: the rich green of the surrounding forest and meadows, the alternating bands of deep red and cobalt that run through the cliffs, and the bright blue of the lake.

The hike itself ranks among the finest. This trail skirts beaver ponds, crosses several meadows, passes two waterfalls, and has several outstanding viewpoints over the Two Medicine area. Hikers wishing to linger may camp near Cobalt Lake and day hike

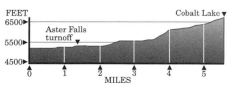

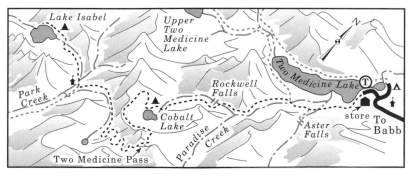

Rockwell Falls

or backpack on over the high alpine ridge crests of Two Medicine Pass to the isolation of Lake Isabel.

Access: At the town of East Glacier Park, head north on Highway 49 for 4 miles. Turn left at the Two Medicine Road and drive 7.9 miles to the end of the road. Park near the store (elevation 5,164 feet).

The hike: Walk past the boat dock and boathouse, then head into the forest on the South Shore Trail. After a brief climb the trail levels off and begins threading its way around beaver ponds and through grassy meadows along the base of Appistoki Peak. After just 0.2 mile the trail divides and a well-used spur goes to the right, heading out to Paradise Point. A half mile beyond, a spur trail branches left for a 0.1-mile side trip to Aster Falls.

At 2.4 miles, the Cobalt Lake Trail leaves the South Shore Trail and heads left, up Paradise Creek valley. Walk along the flanks of Sinopah Mountain to reach Cobalt Creek and Rockwell Falls at 3.5 miles. At this point you

A yellow glacier lily

leave the valley and head up the hillside on a series of easy switchbacks.

Before long, Two Medicine Lake and the sun-dried slopes of Spot Mountain and Two Medicine Ridge come into view. The forest gives way to huckleberry fields, where the berries provide both hikers and bears with tasty snacks in late August.

At 5.7 miles the trail arrives at 6,570-foot Cobalt Lake. The backcountry camp is located to the left and great picnic sites are scattered all along the shore. If you have an excess of time and energy, continue on up to 7,400-foot Two Medicine Pass, located just 2.2 miles above the lake. The pass has a commanding view over Paradise Park and the Park Creek drainage.

To reach the beautiful Lake Isabel, continue down the south side of Two Medicine Pass, descending steadily for 3.8 miles. The Park Creek Trail is reached shortly before crossing Park Creek (4,780 feet). There is a patrol cabin and campsite here. Go right and head up valley a final 2.4 miles to Lake Isabel and the camp area (5,700 feet).

■ ■ ■ ■

25. UPPER TWO MEDICINE LAKE

From Pray Lake outlet
DAY HIKE OR BACKPACK
Round trip: 9.4 miles (14.8 km)
Elevation gain: 370 feet (113 m)
High point: 5,480 feet (1,670 m)
Hiking time: 5 hours
Hikeable: July through mid-October
Difficulty: easy
Maps: USGS Squaw Mountain and Mt. Rockwell

From Upper Boat Dock
DAY HIKE OR BACKPACK
Round trip: 4.4 miles (7 km)
Elevation gain: 320 feet (98 m)
High point: 5,480 feet (1,670 m)
Hiking time: 2½ hours
Hikeable: early July through August
Difficulty: easy
Map: USGS Mt. Rockwell

The hike to Upper Two Medicine Lake offers an excellent opportunity for groups of all ages and energy levels to enjoy a taste of the backcountry for either the day or on an overnight backpack. Along the route hikers will experience a cool forest walk with a side trip to Twin Falls. At the upper lake there is a place to splash for the young and a tremendous view for the older and more reflective minds. Overnight hikers will have the extra

The Sinopah, *docked at the lower end of Two Medicine Lake*

pleasure of watching the brook trout jumping and counting a million stars after sunset.

For little feet, and many older ones, a ride on the tour boat will add immeasurable pleasure to the hike, as well as reduce the distance the packs must be carried. The tour boat, called the *Sinopah,* takes about 30 minutes to reach the Upper Boat Dock.

Access: Hikers planning to walk the entire distance will find the trail by driving through the Two Medicine Campground to the hikers' parking area at the outlet of Pray Lake (elevation 5,170 feet). If you plan to ride the tour boat up the lake, drive to the end of the road and park near the boat dock. Purchase tickets at the boat.

The hike: Cross Two Medicine Creek on a wide bridge and walk 100 feet to a junction. Go left on the North Shore Trail.

After winding through the forest for 3 miles, the trail divides. The Dawson Pass Trail to No Name Lake takes off to the right; stay to the left for Upper Two Medicine Lake. Just 0.1 mile farther is a second junction, this one with the trail from the Upper Boat Dock. Stay to the right and walk 0.2 mile to a third junction, with the trail to Twin Falls, a short and easy side trip.

The trail continues through forest interspersed with occasional fields of huckleberries. Make plenty of noise and watch for bears in the late summer.

Twin Falls, at the upper end of Two Medicine Lake

At 4.7 miles the trail arrives at Upper Two Medicine Lake. Pumpelly Pillar and Mount Helen soar above the north shore. On the south side the rocky slopes of Rising Bull Ridge climb high above the emerald waters, and at the upper end of the lake Lone Walker Mountain dominates the skyline.

■ ■ ■ ■

26. DAWSON PASS LOOP

BACKPACK
Loop trip: 15.4 miles (24.6 km)
Elevation gain: 2,916 feet (889 m)
High point: 8,080 feet (2,463 m)
Hiking time: 2–3 days
Hikeable: August through September
Difficulty: strenuous
Maps: USGS Squaw Mountain, Cut Bank Pass, and Mt. Rockwell

Enjoy an eagle's-eye view of four valleys from one of the most scenic stretches of high alpine trail in Glacier National Park. This loop is a must for all backpackers.

The loop begins and ends at the Two Medicine Campground. The optimum itinerary for the hike would be to walk to Oldman Lake the first night, then either complete the loop the following day or spend the second night at No Name Lake, Upper Two Medicine Lake, or even Cobalt Lake. This schedule allows hikers to make the best use of the terrain and trails. However, this is a popular loop and it is often difficult to get a backcountry camping permit. Be flexible with your itinerary; this trip is worth it.

Access: From the park entrance station on Lower Two Medicine Lake, drive Two Medicine Road 4.5 miles to the Two Medicine Lake Campground. Go right, passing a small ranger's office, and drive through the camp area to find the hikers' parking area at the lower end of Pray Lake (elevation 5,163 feet).

The hike: To begin the loop, walk across the Two Medicine Creek bridge and continue on for 100 feet to an intersection. Go

Fossilized algae form distinctive patterns in sandstone near Dawson Pass

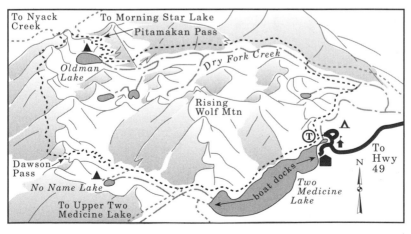

right on a trail that contours around the flanks of Rising Wolf Mountain, then descends into Dry Fork Valley. At 1.8 miles cross the aptly named Dry Fork Creek, then go left and continue up the valley.

At 5 miles the trail divides. Oldman Lake and camp area are located 0.5 mile to the left (6,640 feet). Note that the forest floor near the camp area has a thick covering of huckleberries; watch for bears in the late summer.

From Oldman Lake it is only 1.6 miles and a few steep switchbacks to the 7,580-foot summit of Pitamakan Pass. The climb continues above the pass as the trail traverses open slopes, passing intersections with the trail to Morning Star Lake in the Cut Bank area and the trail to Cut Bank Pass and Nyack Creek. After gaining 500 feet in 0.7 mile, you reach the 8,080-foot trip high point at the Pitamakan Pass overlook.

The overlook marks the start of an incredibly scenic section of alpine trail that contours around Mount Morgan to a narrow pass, then traverses the side of Flinsch Peak to a rocky shoulder overlooking Dawson Pass.

The trail descends on excellently graded switchbacks for 400 feet to 7,598-foot Dawson Pass, then plummets down the rocky hillside for 1.2 miles to the No Name Lake intersection. Continuing down, the rate of descent slackens for the final mile to the upper end of Two Medicine Lake.

Hiker above Oldman Lake

To complete the loop, walk the forested North Shore Trail for a final 3.1 miles along Two Medicine Lake to the campground. Or, walk over to the Upper Boat Dock and let the *Sinopah* carry you and your pack for 2 miles down the lake.

■ ■ ■ ■

27. FIREBRAND PASS

DAY HIKE
Round trip: 9.4 miles (14.8 km)
Elevation gain: 1,867 feet (569 m)
High point: 6,951 feet (2,119 m)
Hiking time: 5 hours
Hikeable: July through mid-October
Difficulty: moderate
Map: USGS Squaw Mountain

During the fire of 1910, a burning ember blew from the fire burning on the west side of the pass, over the crest, and set the east side ablaze. Since that time, the name Firebrand has stuck. The forest has been slow to return to the high alpine country around Firebrand Pass, and the views are unobstructed except by sturdy old tree trunks bleached white by time, ghosts of the old forest.

The Firebrand Pass trail lies in the southeast section of Glacier National Park. This is a relatively pristine area, having escaped the mobs that flock to

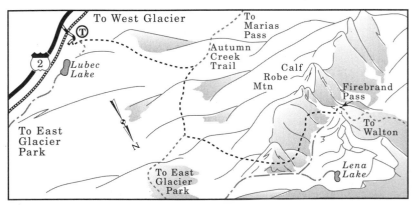

Trail to Firebrand Pass

other parts of the park. The views in this area are fascinating. Looking east one can see the foothills of the Rocky Mountains sloping down to a vast prairie that extends far beyond the visible horizon. In the fall this is an excellent location to look for elk or to listen to the bulls trying out the strength of their bugling calls.

Access: Drive Highway 2 east from Marias Pass for 5.2 miles or west from the town of East Glacier Park for 6.4 miles. The unsigned turnoff is on the northwest side of the highway. There are two dirt access roads, so if you miss the first you can catch the second. The road descends and crosses the railroad tracks; the trailhead is 20 feet beyond the track (elevation 5,084 feet).

The hike: Use the hikers' access to pass through the fence that marks the national park boundary, then follow an old road around a couple of beaver ponds. At 0.2 mile the trail takes off on the left, crosses a grassy field, then heads up the forested hillside, paralleling Coonsa Creek.

The first of two intersections is reached at 1.7 miles. Go right on Autumn Creek Trail and traverse along the base of the mountains. Watch for prints, trails, and other signs of elk in the meadows and along the creeks in this area.

The second intersection is reached at 2.2 miles (5,540 feet). Go left on the Firebrand Pass trail and begin the climb to the pass. At the end of the first ascent, your breath will be coming in gasps. Not to worry; the trail soon settles into a steady and much more comfortable rate of climb. Contour around Calf Robe Mountain, then enter a subalpine basin at the base of the pass.

The trail climbs, traversing the talus slopes, to reach the windswept summit of 6,951-foot Firebrand Pass at 4.7 miles. This is wide-open country with opportunities for roaming. With a good map it is a relatively easy cross-country trip to Lena Lake, or the summit of Red Crow Mountain, or over the shoulder of Calf Robe Mountain to find the trail on the other side. A good map can also help you follow the sometimes-sketchy trail for another 3 miles to Ole Lake (5,580 feet).

■ ■ ■ ■

OTHER TRAILS

Cutbank Pass Trail runs from Pitamakan Pass to the difficult-to-access Nyack Wilderness Camping Area. The trail is noted for its steepness.

Ptarmigan in speckled summer plumage

Cut Bank

The North Fork Cut Bank Creek valley is located on the east side of the park between Two Medicine and St. Mary. Mother Nature has done a beautiful job of landscaping this valley, painting the dry hills in brilliant yellows, outlining rocky mountain summits with bold strokes against the deep blue sky, and setting the creek on a meandering path through the forest and the wide, grassy meadows.

Cut Bank is accessed by a 5-mile-long dirt road with no services at the end except a small campground. Most people who use this area come to backpack in the backcountry. All of the day hikes out of Cut Bank are long, with round trips averaging more than 10 miles.

There is a ranger in residence at Cut Bank who can be contacted in case of an emergency. Backcountry hiking permits are not issued here. The campground has nineteen sites, pit toilets, and running water. Trailers and large units are not recommended.

CUT BANK TRAIL FINDER

Trail Number and Destination	Difficulty	Lowland Lakes	Alpine Lakes	Waterfalls	Scenic Views	Wildlife	Fishing	Backpacking
28 Triple Divide Pass	strenuous	●			●			●
Medicine Grizzly Lake	easy		●					
Pitamakan Lake	strenuous		●					
Pitamakan Pass	strenuous				●			
Morning Star Lake	strenuous		●					●

Atlantic Creek trail near Triple Divide Pass

■ ■ ■ ■

28. TRIPLE DIVIDE PASS

DAY HIKE OR BACKPACK
Round trip: 14.2 miles (22.7 km)
Elevation gain: 2,227 feet (679 m)
High point: 7,397 feet (2,254 m)
Hiking time: 7 hours
Hikeable: mid-July through September
Difficulty: strenuous
Maps: USGS Cut Bank Pass and Mt. Stimson

Triple Divide Pass is as close as you can get by trail to Triple Divide Peak, one of the most unusual points on the North American continent. Triple Divide is a triangular peak that serves as the meeting point for three major watersheds. A drop of water on the summit of Triple Divide Peak could roll west, down the Pacific Creek drainage, to find its way to the Columbia River and on to the Pacific Ocean. Or, a gust of wind might push that droplet north, where it would descend to the St. Mary River and end up in Hudson Bay. Or, a mountain goat might come along and step on the droplet and send it down the Atlantic Creek drainage to the Missouri River and the Gulf of Mexico.

Most hikers would love to stand on the summit of Triple Divide Peak and empty a water bottle just to watch the water start its journey to three different oceans. However, steep rock walls and junky rock preclude all but skilled climbers from ascending the peak. Hikers must be satisfied with Triple Divide

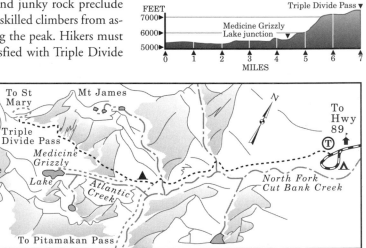

Upper basin of Hudson Bay Creek from Triple Divide Pass

Pass and finding a point where water will flow equally toward the Gulf of Mexico and Hudson Bay.

Access: From St. Mary drive Highway 89 south for 15 miles, then head west on the dirt-surfaced Cut Bank Road for 5 miles to the trailhead (elevation 5,170 feet).

The hike: The trail heads up the valley, paralleling the North Fork Cut Bank Creek while passing through forest interspersed with grassy meadows. When the first intersection is reached at 3.9 miles, only 160 feet of elevation have been gained.

Bighorn sheep

At the intersection, the trail divides. The Pitamakan Pass Trail goes left, climbing to Morning Star Lake and Pitamakan Pass. The Triple Divide Trail follows the right fork and heads up the Atlantic Creek valley. After 0.4 mile the trail passes the forested Atlantic Creek backcountry camp area. There are four tent spaces here, and campfires are allowed.

Just 0.2 mile above the camp area, the trail to Medicine Grizzly Lake branches off on the left, heading up the valley for another nearly level 1.2 miles to the lakeshore. Triple Divide Pass Trail goes to the right.

The final 2.6 miles to the pass are spent in a long, ascending traverse. The trail grade never seems to vary as it heads straight across the hillside over talus slopes and through the rocky ribs of Mount James. Watch for bighorn sheep on the ledges above the trail. Rocks tumbling down the hillside are frequently a sign that sheep are above, even if you cannot see them.

Triple Divide Pass (7,397 feet) is reached 7.1 miles from the Cut Bank trailhead. The pass is surrounded by mountains: Norris, Split, Triple Divide, Razoredge, Medicine Grizzly, and James, to name just a few.

■ ■ ■ ■

OTHER TRAILS

Medicine Grizzly Lake. An easy 11.4-mile round-trip hike to the head of Atlantic Creek leads to a lake in a scenic valley between Medicine Grizzly Peak, Razoredge Mountain, and Triple Divide Peak. The nearest campsite is at Atlantic Creek.

Morning Star Lake. A 13.2-mile round-trip hike up the North Fork Cut Bank Creek leads to a campsite at the subalpine Morning Star Lake. The trail gains only 560 feet from Cut Bank to the lake, making it an easy hike. Morning Star Lake is within easy hiking distance of Pitamakan Lake and Pitamakan Pass.

St. Mary

S St. Mary is much more than just the stop sign at the eastern end of the Going-to-the-Sun Road; it is an area that encompasses all the geographical features that bear the St. Mary name. And the list of St. Marys is impressive: a waterfall, a river, two lakes—one 10 miles long and the other 6 miles long—a glacier-carved valley, a campground, a visitor center, a town, and innumerable scenic viewpoints and stunning vistas.

ST. MARY TRAIL FINDER

Trail Number and Destination	Difficulty	Features						
		Lowland Lakes	Alpine Lakes	Waterfalls	Scenic Views	Wildlife	Fishing	Backpacking
29 Sun Point	easy	●			●		●	
29 St. Mary Falls	easy			●			●	
29 Sunrift Gorge	easy			●				
30 Red Eagle Lake	easy	●			●	●	●	●
31 Otokomi Lake	moderate		●					●
32 Virginia Falls	easy	●		●	●		●	
33 Gunsight Lake	moderate		●	●	●		●	●
34 Siyeh Pass	strenuous				●			
35 Piegan Pass	moderate				●	●		

Lake Ellen Wilson with Gunsight Pass in the distance

ACCOMMODATIONS AND SERVICES

The town of St. Mary lies outside the park boundary, and the motels and the St. Mary Lodge are private enterprises. The Rising Sun Motor Inn, located 6 miles west of town on the Going-to-the-Sun Road, is inside the park and run by Glacier Park, Inc. Guests at the Rising Sun Motor Inn can buy meals at the coffee shop and snack bar or drive to St. Mary and dine at one of the town's informal eateries.

The park has two campgrounds in the vicinity of St. Mary Lake: Rising Sun Campground, which has 83 sites, and St. Mary Campground, which has 156 sites. Evening campfire programs are a feature of the Rising Sun area. Guests at St. Mary Campground can walk to the visitor center for a nightly slide show. In July and August, Rising Sun Campground is full by noon; St. Mary Campground is usually full by dinnertime. Outside the park, there are four privately operated campgrounds in the town of St. Mary and along the shores of Lower St. Mary Lake.

Some groceries and an endless variety of tee shirts can be purchased at the Rising Sun camp store. A more complete selection of souvenirs is available in town. A limited supply of groceries is available at St. Mary. The town also has two gas stations.

Showers are available through the Rising Sun Motor Inn, and tokens are purchased at the camp store. There is a small Laundromat in St. Mary, located in an unmarked building across from the lodge. Be sure to bring your own change and detergent.

A scenic cruise on St. Mary Lake is a popular way to see the area's spectacular scenery. The boat dock is located just west of the Rising Sun area, and the cruise lasts for an hour and a half with an optional 15-minute walk to Baring Falls. Some cruises can be combined with a 2-hour, naturalist-led walk to St. Mary Falls.

The 1913 ranger station is an interesting place to visit. It is located at the Red Eagle Lake trailhead (Hike 30). The old ranger station has been refurbished and is now a museum of life in the park in the early 1900s. The buildings are opened to the public on special occasions, but most of the time visitors must be satisfied with peering in the windows.

■ ■ ■ ■

29. ST. MARY AREA SHORT HIKES

Sun Point. This 1-mile loop trip on a self-guided nature trail begins at the Sun Point picnic area, 9 miles west of St. Mary. Walk out to the point for a view of the lake, then follow the lakeshore trail to the former site of the Going-to-the-Sun chalets.

St. Mary Falls. A 1.6-mile round trip takes you to a beautiful falls. Drive the Going-to-the-Sun Road 10.9 miles west of the St. Mary Entrance Station and park on the left side of the road.

Sunrift Gorge. This 200-foot round-trip walk is a steep climb to a deep, narrow gorge. Baring Creek cuts deeply into a fault fracture, and the resulting narrow passageway is a favorite with photographers. The gorge is located 10.4 miles west of the St. Mary Entrance Station on the Going-to-the-Sun Road. You may also walk down for 0.3 mile from the gorge to Baring Falls.

St. Mary Lake from Wild Goose Island

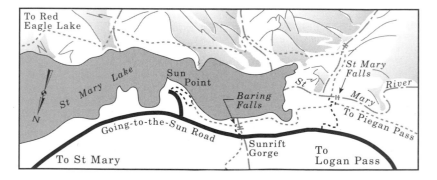

■ ■ ■ ■

30. RED EAGLE LAKE

DAY HIKE OR BACKPACK
Round trip: 15.4 miles (24.6 km)
Elevation gain: 300 feet (91 m)
High point: 4,840 feet (1,475 m)
Hiking time: 7 hours
Hikeable: mid-June through mid-October
Difficulty: easy
Map: USGS Rising Sun

The miles of grassy meadows, which provide habitat for herds of elk and deer—and an occasional mountain lion—make this a unique hike in Glacier National Park.

Red Eagle Lake is a popular destination with day hikers, who come to enjoy the scenery of this glacier-carved valley; with backpackers, who pause there on the widely used, 23.2-mile traverse between St. Mary and Cut Bank; and with fishermen, who throng to this lake, carrying inflatable rafts on their backs, to try their luck with the feisty cutthroats.

Note: The bridges are dismantled in the winter. If you plan to hike here in early summer or after the middle of September, check at any park visitor center or backcountry office before starting out.

Access: From the Highway 89 turnoff at the town of St. Mary, drive 0.3 mile toward the St. Mary Entrance Station. Turn left and follow the signs to the trailhead (elevation 4,540 feet).

The hike: There are two ways to begin the hike. The standard method is to follow the Red Eagle Lake Trail along an abandoned road that takes you up from the shores of St. Mary Lake to a grassy plateau.

The alternative method is to start the trip by following a less-used trail that begins directly behind the 1913 ranger station and climbs through forest to join the main trail at 1.2 miles.

At 3.8 miles the road ends and a trail continues on, dropping down a steep bank into the Red Eagle Creek valley. Once the creek is crossed on a suspension bridge, the trail heads up valley, traversing meadows and forest. A mile later the trail divides. Follow the left fork, which recrosses Red Eagle Creek on a second suspension bridge.

The final 2.9 miles pass quickly as the trail continues to traverse alternating bands of trees and meadows. Red Eagle Lake (4,722 feet) is reached at 7.7 miles. The backpackers' campsite straddles the trail near the edge of the lake. The second camp area, located at the upper end of the lake, is designed for both horse packer and hiker use. Day hikers will find a gravel beach and rock outcroppings at the lower end of the lake, perfect for picnicking and sunbathing.

Trail through open meadows on the hike to Red Eagle Lake

■ ■ ■ ■

31. OTOKOMI LAKE

DAY HIKE OR BACKPACK
Round trip: 10 miles (16 km)
Elevation gain: 1,900 feet (579 m)
High point: 6,660 feet (2,030 m)
Hiking time: 6 hours
Hikeable: mid-July through September
Difficulty: moderate
Map: USGS Rising Sun

Otokomi Lake leaves a lasting impression of intense color. The lake is located in Rose Basin, and the rock walls surrounding the lake are a deep, dark, throbbing red. Within this red basin bright green highlights of the stunted alpine firs and meadow grass seem to almost glow. Above, the sky can be intensely blue and the lingering patches of snow gleam a blinding white.

Access: From the town of St. Mary, drive the Going-to-the-Sun Road 7.5 miles west to the Rising Sun Resort and Campground. Park at the General Store (elevation 4,560 feet).

The hike: The Otokomi Lake trail starts from the left side of the store and parallels the creek, passing the motel units. Beyond the buildings the route enters the forest, then ascends the hillside for the next mile. The first views come when the trail emerges from the trees to skim along the precipitous edge of the impressive Rose Creek Gorge. The gorge is paralleled until it ends at a large waterfall.

Beyond the gorge, the trail follows the creek as it plunges through a series of intriguing cascades. At about 4 miles there is a sudden descent into a sub-

Otokomi Lake

alpine valley where meadows and huckleberry fields alternate with stands of trees. The trail loses its well-graded quality, and the climbs become steep and abrupt. The head of the valley comes into view, but the lake remains hidden.

At 5 miles the trail drops to a three-site backcountry campground. Day hikers should descend to the creek, then go right to the lakeshore. A boot-beaten path heads around the lake in both directions, allowing hikers to find their own personal picnic sites and rock-skipping areas along the shore.

ROCK COLORS

The intense and strikingly varied colors of the parks' rocky hillsides are just one of the many components that make this area so incredibly scenic. Although the majority of the hills and rocks are an everyday-looking gray, hikers will come across thick bands of dark red or maroon-colored rocks and layers of rich green-colored rocks.

The color of the rocks is determined by the presence or absence of iron. The bright red rocks found along the Grinnell Glacier trail were deposited in a shallow ocean environment where the iron was oxidized by the tidal exposure to the air. Rocks with this coloration often have old ripple marks or ancient mud crack lines.

The rich green-colored rocks were formed in deeper water than the red rocks. Although these rocks contain the same quantities of iron-bearing minerals, they did not have the same exposure to oxygen and the amount of oxidization was limited. Look for fossil algae in the green rocks. These rocks can be found at Otokomi Lake at the lakeshore level; above are the red cliffs of the oxidized rocks.

The dark-colored rocks found at the upper end of Lake McDonald and around Trout Lake are the result of subjecting the red and green iron-rich rocks to heat and pressure. These rocks are visible along McDonald Creek on the Sacred Dancing Cascade Loop.

Ripple marks on dark red rock

■   ■   ■   ■

32. VIRGINIA FALLS

DAY HIKE
Round trip: 6 miles (9.6 km)
Elevation gain: 300 feet (91 m)
High point: 4,800 feet (1,463 m)
Hiking time: 3 hours
Hikeable: July through September
Difficulty: easy
Maps: USGS Rising Sun and Logan Pass

This forested hike to three waterfalls is a great way to spend a warm afternoon. Bathe your feet in a creek, cool your face in the spray, or just sit in the shade and let the water and the world rush by.

Access: The hike has two access points. The true start is from Sun Point, located 9.6 miles west of the St. Mary Entrance Station on the Going-to-the-Sun Road. The second is a shortcut access that begins at a small turnout 10.9 miles west of the St. Mary Entrance Station. This access bypasses Baring Falls.

The hike: From Sun Point, follow the nature trail along the shore of St. Mary Lake. Take time to walk out on the point, where a location-finder sign names all the major peaks. The trail heads up the lake, passing the site of the old Going-to-the-Sun chalets, then passes over the low cliffs that line the rocky shore.

At 0.7 mile the trail divides. The right fork heads up 0.3 mile to Sunrift Gorge. If you haven't explored the deep, narrow channel cut by Baring Creek, this is a highly recommended side trip. A few

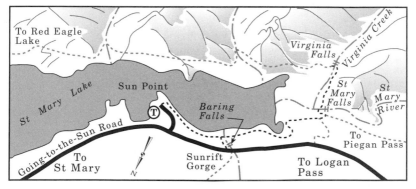

Virginia Falls

feet past the intersection is Baring Falls, the least spectacular and most accessible of the three falls. Beyond the falls, the trail returns briefly to the lakeshore and the site of the tour boat dock, then heads back into the shade of a thick lodgepole forest.

At 1.7 miles the shortcut access trail from the Going-to-the-Sun Road joins on the right. A few feet beyond is another intersection; stay left. The thundering roar of water signals your arrival at St. Mary Falls, 2.5 miles from Sun Point. Here the St. Mary River is crossed on a wide bridge, and hikers may linger in the refreshing mist.

The trail continues to wind through the forest, climbing steadily along cascading Virginia Creek for the final 0.5 mile to Virginia Falls. The falls is visible from the trail; however, if you want to bathe your feet in the clear pool at its base, scramble up the rough path along the right-hand side of the creek. An outhouse is located on the main trail, across the footbridge.

■ ■ ■ ■

33. GUNSIGHT LAKE

Gunsight Lake
DAY HIKE OR BACKPACK
Round trip: 12.6 miles (20.2 km)
Elevation gain: 1,040 feet in; 640 feet out (317 m in; 195 m out)
High point: 5,680 feet (1,731 m)
Hiking time: 6 hours
Hikeable: July through September
Difficulty: moderate
Map: USGS Logan Pass
Lake Mcdonald
BACKPACK
One way: 19.8 miles (32 km)
Elevation gain: 3,966 feet (1,209 m)
High point: 7,360 feet (2,243 m)
Hiking time: 2–3 days
Hikeable: August through September
Difficulty: strenuous
Maps: USGS Logan Pass, Lake McDonald East, and Lake McDonald
West

Gunsight Lake is not only a popular day hike, but also part of the well-known traverse between St. Mary Lake and Lake McDonald. Hikers making the traverse can leave their cars at the Lake McDonald Lodge, ride the shuttle bus to the trailhead, and still have plenty of time to reach

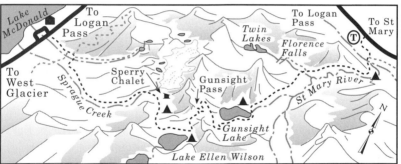

Gunsight Lake with Gunsight Pass in the distance

the first night's camp at Gunsight Lake.

Access: The hike begins at the Jackson Glacier turnout (elevation 5,280 feet) on the Going-to-the-Sun Road, 13.2 miles west of the St. Mary Entrance Station or 4.9 miles east of Logan Pass.

The hike: The hike begins with a heartbreaking descent in which 640 feet of elevation is lost in 1.5 miles. The descent ends when the trail reaches Deadwood Falls and the intersection with the St. Mary Lake Trail.

From the intersection, go straight across Reynolds Creek, past a small campsite reserved for Continental Divide Trail hikers, then head up the St. Mary River valley. The base of the valley is wide and swampy, ideal habitat for deer and elk, and the climb is very gradual.

At 4.3 miles a spur trail to Florence Falls branches off on the right. Shortly beyond this intersection, you leave the forest and begin a traverse across the brushy flanks of Fusillade Mountain. Views of glaciers and mountains (Citadel, Logan, Blackfoot, and Jackson) fill the horizon. Below, Siksika Falls glistens brightly in the dark forest. At 6.2 miles there is a gradual descent, which ends in 0.1 mile at the lakeshore and a backcountry campsite (5,680 feet).

Hikers continuing on to Lake McDonald must cross the outlet of Gunsight

Lake and follow the trail over the high alpine tundra for another 2.8 miles to 6,946-foot Gunsight Pass. (*Note:* The bridge over the outlet stream is removed in September; check with the ranger before starting out.) Hikers who linger at the pass may find themselves the center of attention for squirrels looking for handouts and mountain goats looking for salt.

From Gunsight Pass follow the trail another 4.4 miles, passing a campsite at Lake Ellen Wilson, to Glacier Basin, where the Sperry Campground and Sperry Chalet are located. The final 6.4 miles of the traverse are a forested descent to Lake McDonald (Hike 6).

■ ■ ■ ■

34. SIYEH PASS

DAY HIKE
Round trip: 9.4 miles (15 km)
Elevation gain: 2,390 feet (723 m)
High point: 8,240 feet (2,512 m)
Hiking time: 6 hours
Hikeable: mid-July through mid-September
Difficulty: strenuous
Maps: USGS Logan Pass and Rising Sun

Meadows, lakes, and alpine views are the main attractions of this hike through some of the highest country traversed by trail in Glacier National Park

Siyeh Pass may be hiked as a round trip from Siyeh Bend or as a one-way excursion ending at Sunrift Gorge. The one-way option is 10.3 miles (16.5 km) long and you must arrange your own transportation back to the trailhead or walk another mile east along St. Mary Lake to catch the shuttle bus at Sun Point. (Ranger-led walks of this trail include a carpool; check at the St. Mary Visitor Center for details.)

Access: Drive or ride the shuttle bus to Siyeh Bend, located 15.6 miles west of the town of St. Mary on the Going-to-the-Sun Road. (From the opposite direction, Siyeh Bend is located 3 miles east of Logan Pass.) The hike begins at the center of the bend, across the road from the parking area (elevation 5,850 feet).

The hike: The Siyeh Bend Cutoff Trail begins by paralleling Siyeh Creek but soon heads uphill into the forest. At 1.5 miles (6,260 feet), the cutoff trail ends. Go left on the Piegan Pass trail and head north through alternating bands of meadows and trees. This is grizzly bear habitat, so watch for tracks and scat and make plenty of noise, whether you see any sign of bears or not.

At 2.8 miles the trail divides; the left fork continues on to Many Glacier.

Sexton Glacier

Go right on the trail to Siyeh Pass and head into Preston Park, a beautiful sub-alpine area of small lakes and open meadows. Take time to wander around one of these ponds to catch a view of Piegan, Heavy Runner, and Reynolds Mountains reflected in the shallow waters.

At the upper end of Preston Park, leave the meadows and

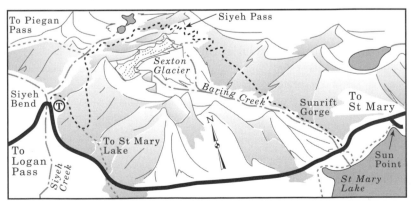

switchback up the rocky talus slopes. The trail reaches 7,750-foot Siyeh Pass and continues to climb barren slopes to an 8,240-foot high point where it levels briefly on a barren talus slope. A 100-foot descent to an unnamed, wind-blasted col marks the turnaround point for hikers heading back to Siyeh Bend.

If you opt to continue down to Sunrift Gorge, there is a long, well-graded descent through open meadows to look forward to. At 0.6 mile below the col, an abandoned trail branches right to Sexton Glacier.

As the descent continues, waterfalls come into view, streaming off the cliffs below the glacier. Eventually these streams flow together and hurtle down the bright red bedrock and into Sunrift Gorge at the Going-to-the-Sun Road.

Any hikers who plan to catch the shuttle at Sun Point must follow the gorge trail under the road and descend for 0.3 mile. Go left at the intersection and walk along the lakeshore for 0.7 mile to Sun Point.

■ ■ ■ ■

35. PIEGAN PASS

Piegan Pass
DAY HIKE
Round trip: 8.8 miles (14 km)
Elevation gain: 1,720 feet (524 m)
High point: 7,570 feet (2,307 m)
Hiking time: 4 hours
Hikeable: mid-July through September
Difficulty: moderate
Map: USGS Logan Pass
Many Glacier
DAY HIKE
One way : 12.8 miles (20.5 km)
Elevation gain: 1,720 feet (524 m)
High point: 7,570 feet (2,307 m)
Hiking time: 7 hours
Hikeable: August through mid-September
Difficulty: strenuous
Maps: USGS Logan Pass and Many Glacier

High alpine splendor of delicate gardens and immense vistas are the certain rewards found along the Piegan Pass trail. Less certain but commonly seen are mountain goats and bighorn sheep that live on the hillsides above and below the pass area.

This popular trail connects the Going-to-the-Sun Road with the Many Glacier area. If you use the shuttle bus and a little imagination, you can create numerous exciting loop hikes.

Access: Drive or ride the shuttle bus to Siyeh Bend, located 15.6 miles west of the town of St. Mary on the Going-to-the-Sun Road. (From Logan Pass drive east, descending 3 miles to find parking on the right side of the road just beyond the bend at 5,850 feet).

The hike: The trail begins next to Siyeh Creek on the opposite side of the road from the parking area. Follow the Siyeh Bend Cutoff trail along the creek for 0.1 mile before heading up the hillside and into the forest, climbing at a steady pace. At 1.2 miles (6,260 feet), the cutoff trail ends. Go left and continue the ascent on the Piegan Pass trail, which traverses north below Mataphi Peak. Through alternating bands of trees and meadows hikers can view Piegan Mountain—with the deeply crevassed Piegan Glacier clinging to its steep slopes.

At 2.8 miles the trail divides in a relatively open area know as Preston Park (7,000 feet). The right fork climbs to Siyeh Pass (Hike 34). Stay left and continue the steady climb.

The vegetation is abruptly left behind at 3.1 miles as the trail begins a nearly level traverse below the rugged spires of Cataract Mountain. Watch for mountain goats and bighorn sheep on the slopes above or below the trail. To the south the massive Jackson and Blackfoot Glaciers dominate the skyline. Ahead is the fortresslike backside of the Garden Wall.

A final, short sprint leads to the summit of Piegan Pass at 4.4 miles (7,570 feet). An old stone structure and tower for a

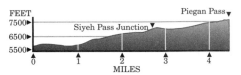

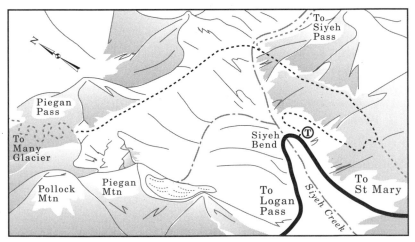

Bighorn sheep on the trail below Piegan Pass

locomotive bell still mar the otherwise perfect high alpine setting. The trail continues on, and so should hikers. Those turning around at the pass should not miss the chance to gaze down Cataract Creek. If heading on, follow the horse trail down into the impressive valley. Near the bottom you may choose to follow the horse trail all the way to the stables at the Swiftcurrent Hotel or leave the main trail at Feather Plume Falls and head to the Swiftcurrent Lake trailhead via Grinnell and Josephine Lakes.

Logan Pass

Logan Pass is the highest point on the Going-to-the-Sun Road, and for many people it is the high point of a visit to Glacier National Park. The pass lies at timberline and has an ideal mixture of subalpine and alpine environments: dwarf trees and verdant meadows. Beautiful fields of flowers lure visitors away from their cars for long walks along the nearby Garden Wall or through the Hanging Gardens. Mountains provide dramatic backdrops for family portraits. Wildlife watching fascinates young and old. Visitors arrive planning to spend an hour at the pass and end up spending all day.

Because Logan Pass is the scenic highlight of the park, it is crowded. From midmorning to late afternoon, finding parking at the summit is difficult to impossible. To avoid parking problems, try to arrive before 10:00 A.M. or after 4:00 P.M., or take the shuttle and avoid parking at the summit altogether.

Logan Pass has a very fragile environment, and the meadows take years to regrow if they are trampled. When walking through the alpine flower fields, stay on the established trail. Do not pick the flowers. Do not feed the ground squirrels, deer, mountain goats, or bighorn sheep that call this area home.

Weather at the pass is unpredictable. In the high alpine environment there is no shelter from the wind and rain. It may even snow in July or August. Your best bet is to bring both warm clothing and sunscreen on every walk.

Bearhat Mountain from Hidden Lake Trail

LOGAN PASS TRAIL FINDER

Trail Number and Destination	Difficulty	Features						
		Lowland Lakes	Alpine Lakes	Waterfalls	Scenic Views	Wildlife	Fishing	Backpacking
36 Hidden Lake	moderate		●		●	●	●	
37 The Garden Wall	strenuous				●	●		●

SERVICES

The Logan Pass Visitor Center is the best place to have your questions answered about places to walk to and types of flowers you will see. The center has a bookstore, exhibits on the alpine environment, rest rooms, and running water.

No food service, lodging, or gas is available at Logan Pass.

■ ■ ■ ■

36. HIDDEN LAKE

Hidden Lake Overlook
DAY HIKE
Round trip: 3 miles (5 km)
Elevation gain: 480 feet (146 m)
High point: 7,130 feet (2,173 m)
Hiking time: 1½ hours
Hikeable: mid-July through September
Difficulty: moderate
Map: USGS Logan Pass

Hidden Lake
DAY HIKE
Round trip: 6 miles (9.6 km)
Elevation gain: 480 feet in; 755 feet out (146 m in; 230 m out)
High point: 7,130 feet (2,173 m)
Hiking time: 4 hours
Hikeable: mid-July through September
Difficulty: moderate
Maps: USGS Logan Pass and Mt. Cannon

No visit to Glacier National Park is complete without a hike on the Hidden Lake Trail. On this short trail hikers explore the elements that are the very essence of the park: the flower-laden meadows, the glaciers, the jagged peaks that form the Garden Wall, the wildlife, and a lake carved by ancient glaciers. It is not necessary to walk the entire distance to get the feel of the area. The meadows begin

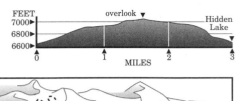

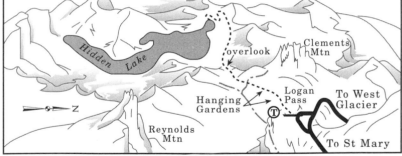

at the trailhead, and so do the views. At a bare minimum, plan to walk the nature loop, located at the trailhead.

Access: Drive or ride the shuttle bus up Going-to-the-Sun Road to the Logan Pass summit parking area (elevation 6,646 feet).

The hike: This hike has two distinct parts. The first half of the hike follows the wide pavement and boardwalk up the hill behind the visitor center. As a result of the trail's popularity and the fragile nature of the meadows it crosses, an intricate boardwalk has been built to keep feet off the delicate hillside. Hikers should stay on the boardwalk as it climbs over the flower-covered terraces of the Hanging Gardens. Once in the meadows, watch for ground squirrels, hoary marmots, and ptarmigan.

The boardwalk ends at the base of Clements Mountain by the edge of an old moraine. The glacier has receded to just a patch of dirty ice; however, the moraine remains in excellent shape, outlining the former boundaries of the ice.

Mountain goat, a common sight at Hidden Lake Overlook

A wide path continues on from the boardwalk, passing several streams and a couple of flower-festooned waterfalls. At 1.2 miles the trail enters Hidden Lake Pass. Turn your binoculars on the lower slopes of Clements Mountain and search for mountain goats, which spend their mornings sunbathing on the ledges above the trail.

At the far end of the pass is the Hidden Lake Overlook. From the viewing platform, it is possible to look down on Hidden Lake and a couple of adjacent tarns, 755 feet below, boxed in by Bearhat Mountain to the west, glacier-covered Gunsight Mountain to the south, and Cannon and Clements Mountains to the north.

The second half of the hike is more peaceful then the first. The trail traverses through meadows below Clements Mountain and Mount Cannon, then switchbacks steeply down to the lakeshore. The clear water tempts many hikers to try a cooling dip. Few swimmers stay in long.

■ ■ ■ ■

37. THE GARDEN WALL

The Loop
DAY HIKE OR BACKPACK
One way: 11.8 miles (18.9 km)
Elevation gain: 800 feet (244 m)
High point: 7,200 feet (2,195 m)
Hiking time: 7 hours
Hikeable: mid-July through September
Difficulty: strenuous
Maps: USGS Logan Pass, Many Glacier, and Ahern Pass

Granite Park Chalet
DAY HIKE OR BACKPACK
Round trip: 15.2 miles (24.3 km)
Elevation gain: 800 feet (244 m)
High point: 7,200 feet (2,195 m)
Hiking time: 8 hours
Hikeable: mid-July through September
Difficulty: strenuous
Maps: USGS Logan Pass and Many Glacier

If you have just one day to devote to hiking in Glacier National Park, walk the Highline Trail along the Garden Wall to Granite Park. On this hike you will walk through flower-covered meadows and glacier-carved basins, past bubbling

Mountain goat with McDonald Creek valley in the background

creeks and views of ice-sculpted mountains. Wildlife abounds, and chances are good of seeing anything from ground squirrels and marmots to mountain goats, bighorn sheep, and, of course, grizzly bears.

There are several ways to approach this hike. If you are in good shape, you can hike the entire distance from Logan Pass to Granite Park and back in one day. The popular alternative is a one-way hike to Granite Park, followed by a descent to The Loop on the Going-to-the-Sun Road. The shuttle bus offers a convenient way to return to the Logan Pass trailhead. A third option is to spend a night at a backcountry campground or at the Granite Park Chalet. However, in July and August, the campsite is open only to hikers on extended trips.

Access: Drive the Going-to-the-Sun Road to Logan Pass and park at the summit (elevation 6,646 feet). The trail begins across the road, opposite the parking lot entrance.

The hike: The hike to Granite Park follows the famous Northern Highline Trail from Logan Pass across the equally well-known Garden Wall. The trail has a spectacular beginning, first traversing the meadows above the road, then cutting across cliffs on a narrow ledge where a garden-hose-covered cable adds security on the exposed sections.

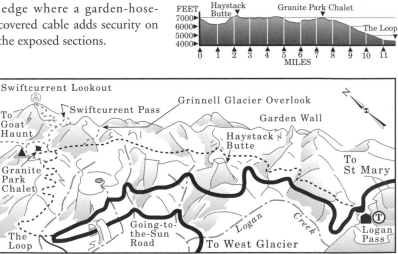

Hikers below Haystack Butte on Northern Highline Trail

At 2.2 miles the trail winds through a glacier-carved basin, then climbs to a small pass between Mount Gould and Haystack Butte. Hikers arriving in this area at midday may have the opportunity to watch the mountain goats on their daily trek from the open slopes of the Garden Wall to the shade of Haystack Butte.

The next couple of miles are spent traversing a steep hillside, passing from one small meadow to the next. The Livingston Range comes into view, as does the Granite Park Chalet. At 6.8 miles pass a spur trail to the Grinnell Glacier Overlook. (The trail climbs 1,000 feet in just 0.8 mile.) At 7.6 miles the trail divides. The right fork ascends to the chalet, and the left fork descends 3.7 miles to The Loop.

■ ■ ■ ■

OTHER TRAILS

Flattop Mountain Trail is frequently used by horse parties to access the Fifty Mountain area. The trail begins at Packers Roost, which is reached by a spur road below The Loop on the Going-to-the-Sun Road. From the trailhead, climb steadily over Flattop Mountain for 5.7 miles to the Flattop Camp area, then on to reach the Fifty Mountain Camp area at 12 miles.

Northern Highline Trail is an alternate name for a 19.5-mile trail that runs from Logan Pass north along the Garden Wall to Granite Park Chalet and the Fifty Mountain Camp area. This trail is often plagued by steep and icy snow slopes until mid-August.

THE SHAPE OF THINGS

The geological history of Glacier and Waterton Lakes National Parks is a fascinating story of how an ocean floor ended up on top of mountains. But the parks we see today were not shaped by the oceans or even by the forces that caused the land to buckle and bend, thrusting older rock strata over younger.

The shaping of the parks occurred recently. About 2 million years ago large sheets of ice covered the lands and massive glaciers flowed down the river valleys. The rasping of the rocks under the heavy ice dug deep trenches, changing the valleys from a V shape to a broader U shape. Most of the lakes in the two parks have an east-west orientation because the ice started at the mountain crests and flowed out.

Lakes such as Bertha and Crypt in Waterton Lakes National Park are called cirque lakes. These were formed by glaciers that descended from the mountains above, only to be cut off by a larger sheet of ice in the main valley. The water descending from these cirques creates many of the spectacular waterfalls seen around the two parks.

The distinctive horn, pillar, or pyramid shapes of the mountains are also the result of glacier carving. Mountains such as Reynolds and Clements, easily viewed at Logan Pass, were carved by glaciers from three or more sides. The knife-edged Garden Wall was the result of glaciers carving on two sides of the ridge at the same time. This shape is known as an arête.

Pyramid-shaped Mount Clements rises above Going-to-the-Sun Road near Logan Pass

Many Glacier

The Indian name for the Swiftcurrent Creek valley means "waterfalls" and the European settlers renamed it Many Glacier, but unless someone can coin a word that encompasses superb alpine scenery; glacier-carved mountains; fifteen lakes; miles of meadows; a profusion of flowers; and an abundance of wildlife, glaciers, and waterfalls, no single word in the English or the Blackfeet languages can adequately describe this area.

Grinnell Lake from the Grinnell Glacier Trail

MANY GLACIER TRAIL FINDER

Trail Number and Destination	Difficulty	Features						
		Lowland Lakes	Alpine Lakes	Waterfalls	Scenic Views	Wildlife	Fishing	Backpacking
38 Apikuni Falls	easy			•				
38 Fishercap Lake	easy	•					•	
39 Swiftcurrent Ridge Lake	moderate	•			•		•	
40 Poia Lake–Redgap Pass Loop	strenuous		•		•			•
41 Cracker Lake	moderate		•					•
42 Cataract Creek Trail	strenuous	•		•	•	•		
43 Grinnell Lake	easy	•			•			
44 Grinnell Glacier	moderate		•		•			
45 Redrock Falls	easy		•	•				
46 Iceberg Lake	moderate		•	•	•			
47 Ptarmigan Tunnel	strenuous		•		•			
48 Swiftcurrent Pass	strenuous		•		•			•
49 The Northern Circle	strenuous		•	•	•	•	•	•
50 Belly River	moderate		•	•	•		•	•
51 Gable Pass and Slide Lake	difficult	•			•		•	•
52 Mokowanis Lake	moderate		•	•	•		•	•
52 Stoney Indian Pass	strenuous		•	•	•			•

ACCOMMODATIONS AND SERVICES

The main accommodations in this area are the huge Many Glacier Hotel, located on the pristine shores of Swiftcurrent Lake, and the Swiftcurrent Motor Inn, with its motel units and rustic cabins. Glacier Park, Inc., runs the hotel and motor inn, which are booked for months ahead (see the Where to Stay section in the Introduction for details). The closest lodging outside the park is a small motel in Babb, Montana, 11 miles to the east.

The Many Glacier Campground is open for full operation from mid-June to late September. Primitive camping, without running water, is allowed in the fall until the area is closed by snow. In midsummer there is a campfire program every night. The campground, which has 112 sites, is usually full by noon in July and August, and late arrivers should plan to spend the night outside the park at one of the two KOA campgrounds on Lower St. Mary Lake.

A small store near the campground has a supply of basic food, camping items, and fishing gear, as well as the usual souvenir assortment. Showers for you and washing machines and dryers for your clothes are available at the Swiftcurrent Motor Inn. Tokens may be purchased at the camp store or the front desk.

Food services are available at the Many Glacier Hotel dining room and snack bar. The Swiftcurrent Motor Inn has a coffee shop.

The Many Glacier Ranger Station, located next to the campground entrance, is open mid-June through late September, from 8:00 A.M. to 4:30 P.M. Backpacking permits are issued there.

Some consider the scenic boat tours at Many Glacier the most entertaining in the park. The boat departs from the Many Glacier Hotel dock and crosses Swiftcurrent Lake. Passengers disembark on the far side of the lake and take a short walk through the forest to Lake Josephine, where a second boat completes the tour. Park naturalists are on board selected trips to point out the scenic highlights and answer questions. Tickets for the boat tours can be purchased at the kiosk located near the Many Glacier Hotel.

Boat-and-hike tours offer a fun and easy way to explore the Many Glacier area. Take the boat to the upper end of Lake Josephine, then head out for a hike by yourself or with a boat guide or a ranger. In July and August there is a special early morning cruise for hikers taking the ranger-led walk to Grinnell Glacier. Rangers also guide two daily walks from the upper boat dock to Grinnell Lake.

Rowboats and canoes are available for rent at the Many Glacier Hotel dock. Private canoes, rowboats, windsurfers, and kayaks may be launched from the east side of Swiftcurrent Lake.

Horseback rides here, starting from the Many Glacier Corral, are among the most scenic in the park. The corral, open from mid-June through mid-September, offers 1-hour, 2-hour, 3-hour, and all-day rides to places such as an old mining community on Cracker Flats, Cracker Lake, Poia Lake, and Granite Park Chalet.

■ ■ ■ ■

38. MANY GLACIER AREA SHORT HIKES

Apikuni Falls. A 1.6-mile round trip on a steep trail with an 880-foot elevation gain leads to a pretty falls located at the edge of alpine meadows. A rough way-trail continues on from the falls, climbing over a band of cliffs to Natahki Lakes, a hike suitable only for the sure-footed. The trail begins at the Grinnell Glacier Exhibit, located 1.1 miles east of the Many Glacier Hotel.

Swiftcurrent Lake. A 2.4-mile self-guided nature trail loops the entire lake. Begin the walk from the south end of Many Glacier Hotel or at the Many Glacier Picnic Area. Pamphlets are available at both trailheads and at the ranger station.

Lake Josephine. This 2-mile round-trip hike, with an elevation gain of just 80 feet, has views of two lakes. Begin at the Many Glacier Picnic Area, located 0.7 mile west of the Many Glacier Hotel. Walk around Swiftcurrent Lake to the first intersection and go right, over a low hill, to the Lake Josephine boat dock, then return the way you came.

Fishercap Lake. A round trip of just 0.5 mile, with only minor elevation

Bull elk

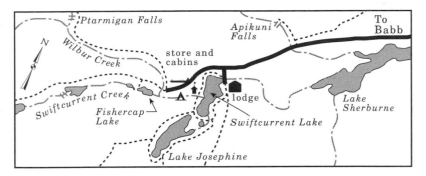

gain, takes you to a lake where moose, elk, and deer are often seen in the early morning or evening. The trail begins at the end of the Many Glacier Road. Follow the Swiftcurrent Pass Trail for 0.1 mile to the lake trail intersection, go left, and descend to the lake. Fishing is reportedly poor.

Ptarmigan Falls. This 5-mile round trip gains only 500 feet of elevation. Meadows, wildflowers, and views make this the most scenic short hike in this area. The trail begins at the end of the Many Glacier Road. Follow the Iceberg Lake–Ptarmigan Lake Trail to the falls.

■ ■ ■ ■

39. SWIFTCURRENT RIDGE LAKE

DAY HIKE
Round trip: 3.2 miles (5.1 km) or 7.5 miles (12 km)
Elevation gain: 1,332 feet (407 m)
High point: 6,080 feet (1,853 m)
Hiking time: 4 hours
Hikeable: June to mid-October
Difficulty: moderate
Map: USGS Lake Sherburne

Swiftcurrent Ridge Lake has two unique features that make it an ideal half-day hike: the first is a stunning view up the Swiftcurrent Creek valley, and the second is the quiet and peacefulness of this rarely visited area.

Access: The official trailhead is located on the north side of the main road to Many Glacier, 10.4 miles beyond the turnoff at Babb, at the Apikuni Falls parking area (elevation 4,880 feet). An alternative, rather steep, shortcut trailhead starts at the Many Glacier Entrance Station, 7.5 miles west of Babb. Park in the lot located just past the entrance station.

Swiftcurrent Ridge Lake

The hike: The official trail to Swiftcurrent Ridge Lake makes a long, climbing traverse across the flanks of the deeply eroded Apikuni Mountain. As the trail heads east, you will glimpse fleeting views of Lake Sherburne in the valley below.

The shortcut trail cuts off 2 miles by swooshing nearly straight up the hillside to intersect the main trail 0.5 mile below Swiftcurrent Ridge Lake. The shortcut trail climbs through open forest and straight up a couple of small, flower-speckled meadows.

The lake lies in a broad bench on

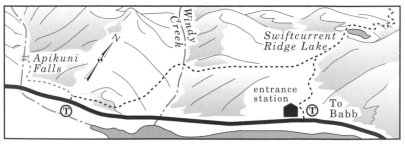

Swiftcurrent Ridge. Water access is limited by dense vegetation along the shores. The best point to reach the lake is found by following the trail around to the north side of the lake.

For stunning views and an ideal picnic site, go right on one of the spur trails that branch off just before the lake. Walk the open ridge crest through a subalpine flower garden to an expansive view of Lake Sherburne and the entire Many Glacier Valley.

■ ■ ■ ■

40. POIA LAKE–REDGAP PASS LOOP

BACKPACK
Loop trip: 27.9 miles (44.6 km)
Elevation gain: 10,552 feet (3,222 m)
High point: 7,520 feet (2,292 m)
Hiking time: 2–3 days
Hikeable: late July through September
Difficulty: strenuous
Maps: USGS Lake Sherburne, Many Glacier, and Gable Mountain

High passes, subalpine lakes, waterfalls, broad vistas, and a tunnel through a nearly perpendicular rock wall combine to create a spectacular hike. The Poia Lake–Redgap Pass leg of the loop is an alternate route for the Continental Divide National Scenic Trail, used in early or late season when the Northern Highline Trail is snowed in.

This is not a perfect loop. The two main trails that make up the loop have separate trailheads, located several miles apart from each other along the Many Glacier Road. Hikers must decide if they want to tackle this short link at the beginning of the hike—and get it over with—or wait until the end to make the dash down the road when the packs are lighter.

A few potential route difficulties may hinder your progress. At times park officials must close the Ptarmigan Tunnel—on the return leg of the loop—because of snow or unsafe conditions. In mid- to late summer, the berries in the broad cirque below the Ptarmigan Wall attract bears, so bear closures are also a possibility. Also, due to the popularity of the area, you may have to wait a day or so until your chosen campsite becomes available.

Access: The official Poia Lake trailhead is located on the north side of the main road to Many Glacier, 10.4 miles beyond the turnoff at Babb, at the Apikuni Falls parking area (elevation 4,880 feet).

The hike: The Poia Lake Trail begins with a well-graded, easterly climbing traverse across the flanks of Apikuni Mountain. At 2.7 miles, pass the shortcut trail from the Many Glacier Entrance Station. Swiftcurrent Ridge Lake is passed at 3.2 miles (6,080 feet). The forested crest of Swiftcurrent Ridge is crossed at 3.4 miles (6,160 feet), followed by a steady descent into the Kennedy Creek valley.

The trail passes several small pocket marshes on the descent before reaching the valley floor at 4.8 miles. Head west, up Kennedy Creek valley, ascending gradually over the rocky hillsides along the occasionally spectacular Kennedy Creek. Poia Lake camp area is reached at 6.3 miles, (5,680 feet). This is usually the first night's stop.

Beyond the campsite, the trail crosses Kennedy Creek above the waterfalls near the Poia Lake outlet, then continues up the north side of the valley. The climb is very gradual for the next 2.5 miles. The trail stays in the brush and forest of the valley floor.

At 9.5 miles from the Many Glacier Road the trail begins the climb to the pass, crossing out of the forest zone, through the subalpine zone, and into the high alpine tundra. Reddish rocks signal that the pass is near.

At 11.9 miles the trail passes a reddish tower, then heads over the top 7,520-foot crest of Redgap Pass to a dramatic view west to Mount Merrit. Beyond the pass, the trail descends into the Belly River area. After 2.5 miles of descent, the Redgap Pass Trail meets the trail from Ptarmigan Tunnel. Go right and descend to the second night's campsite at Lower Lake Elizabeth (4,892 feet), reached at the 16.4-mile point.

The 9.9-mile hike from Lake Elizabeth back to Many Glacier is extremely scenic. From the lake, the trail climbs with nonstop determination for 4.9 miles. Ptarmigan Tunnel (7,200 feet), is a destination of many day hikers (see

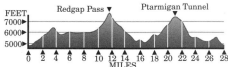

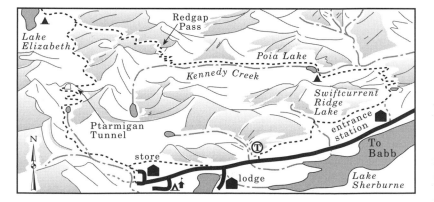

Waterfall on Kennedy Creek at the Poia Lake outlet

Hike 47). Once through the tunnel, the trail descends, passing Ptarmigan Lake and Ptarmigan Falls.

As you near the valley floor, 9.7 miles from Lake Elizabeth, turn left and head down valley on Trail 152. This trail contours along the hillside. When the trail ends, walk along the side of the road to reach Apikuni Falls trailhead and the starting point at 27.9 miles.

■ ■ ■ ■

41. CRACKER LAKE

DAY HIKE OR BACKPACK
Round trip: 11.2 miles (17.9 km)
Elevation gain: 1,140 feet (347 m)
High point: 5,950 feet (1,658 m)
Hiking time: 6 hours
Hikeable: mid-July through September
Difficulty: moderate
Maps: USGS Many Glacier, Swiftcurrent Lake, and Logan Pass

The turquoise blue color of Cracker Lake is startling in its intensity. On a cloudy day, the lake water has an iridescent glow that seems to fill the entire basin. On clear days, the color is so deep and rich that the lake looks like stained glass.

In a park with more than 250 lakes, Cracker Lake ranks as one of the most eye-catching. It is sandwiched between cliffs that rise 3,000 feet in a single pitch.

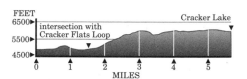

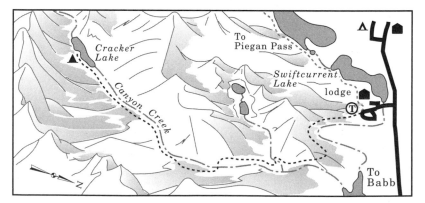

Cracker Lake

Waterfalls lace the hillsides, and delicate meadows surround the lake with a few clumps of stunted subalpine firs to complete the scene.

Access: From the Highway 89 intersection at Babb, drive the Many Glacier Road 11.4 miles and go left at the Many Glacier Hotel turnoff. Go left again when the road divides. Park near the horse corral (elevation 4,890 feet).

The hike: Walk to the end of the parking lot to find the trailhead. After 50 feet the trail divides; the Piegan Pass Trail continues straight and the Cracker Lake Trail goes to the left and descends gradually to the muddy shores of Lake Sherburne.

Once the Cracker Lake Trail reaches lake level, it begins a gradual climb along the edge of Cracker Flats. A horse trail branches off left at 1.5 miles to loop through the flats around an old mining townsite. The crossing of Allen Creek at 1.7 miles marks the beginning of the climb into the Canyon Creek valley on a series of well-graded switchbacks. The next landmark is Canyon Creek, which is crossed at 3.5 miles.

The climb continues, gradually but steadily, through a thinning forest. At 5.6 miles the trail reaches the lake and divides. Stay left along the east side of the lake to reach the backcountry camp area. Shortly beyond, the trail passes some old machinery, abandoned by workmen at the Cracker Mine. The mine shaft is still there, but it is very dangerous to enter. You can walk all the way around the lake traversing the open meadows and grassy hillsides, then cross Canyon Creek at the lake outlet to return to the main trail.

■ ■ ■ ■

42. CATARACT CREEK TRAIL

DAY HIKE
Round trip: 16.6 miles (27 km)
Elevation gain: 2,682 feet (819 m)
High point: 7,570 feet (2,308 m)
Hiking time: 8 hours
Hikeable: August through mid-September
Difficulty: strenuous
Maps: USGS Many Glacier and Logan Pass

This invigorating trail takes hikers from the green forests and aqua blue lakes of the Many Glacier valley to the stark, almost monochromic high alpine world on the ridge crests at the edge of the sky. The pass area is often shared with mountain goats and bighorn sheep.

Trailheads to Piegan Pass are located at Many Glacier and on the Going-to-the-Sun Road (Hike 35). The Going-to-the Sun Road trailhead is the easier access, with excellent scenery. The trail from the Many Glacier side up Cataract Creek is the longer climb with exceptional views. Lakes and waterfalls help blunt the pain of the climb. There are no campsites on this trail, so the entire trip must be completed in a single day.

Access: Drive the Many Glacier Road 11.4 miles west from the Highway 89 intersection at Babb. Go left at the Many Glacier Hotel turnoff and left again when the road divides. Park near the horse corral (elevation 4,890 feet).

The hike: Walk to the south end of the parking lot to find the Piegan Pass–Cracker Lake trailhead on the left. After 50 feet the trail divides; stay right on Trail 113. The trail skirts along the base of Allen Mountain, then contours the forested hillside above Lake Josephine, gaining little elevation. The main points to look for along this portion of the trail are the connector trails that descend

Cataract Creek valley from Piegan Pass

to Lake Josephine at 1.3 miles and 2.3 miles. At 4 miles pass the Feather Plume connecter trail, a few feet from the delicate falls. This intersection marks the start of the true climb to the pass.

The Cataract Creek Trail heads up the talus, crossing and recrossing Cataract Creek as it ascends the steep slope along

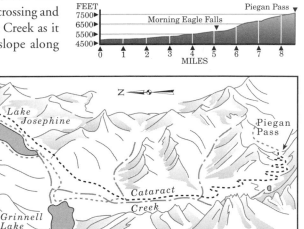

the backside of the Garden Wall. The massive cliffs are much more impressive on this side. Near 5.3 miles, the trail reaches the base of Morning Eagle Falls. Switchbacks are the order of the day as the trail continues its headlong assault on the pass. It takes 3 more miles to reach the 7,570-foot summit of Piegan Pass. Views expand as you climb. At first Angel Wing dominates the skyline, then the Garden Wall soars above, casting deep shadow over the valley below.

Piegan Pass is a narrow cut between Piegan Mountain, neighboring Pollock Mountain, and Cataract Mountain. Look carefully on the surrounding slopes for mountain goats and on the pocket meadows beyond the pass for bighorn sheep.

On the return trip, consider taking the Feather Plume cutoff and returning via Grinnell Lake and Trail 171, which runs along the south shore of Lake Josephine and the aptly named Stump Lake before rejoining the Piegan Pass Trail near the parking lot.

■ ■ ■ ■

43. GRINNELL LAKE

DAY HIKE
Round trip: 6.8 miles (10.9 km)
Elevation gain: 272 feet (88 m)
High point: 4,950 feet (1,509 m)
Hiking time: 4 hours
Hikeable: July through mid-October
Difficulty: easy
Map: USGS Many Glacier

When hiking to Grinnell Lake, you can choose between a cool walk through the shady forest or a scenic traverse over rocky avalanche slopes with views of the entire valley. Or you can be creative and mix the two routes to make interesting combinations, such as a loop hike or a crazy figure eight.

If you prefer a lazy day, with more basking in the sun at the lakeshore than walking, ride the tour boats up Swiftcurrent Lake and Lake Josephine. The resulting hike from the upper end of Lake Josephine is a 1.8-mile round trip with virtually no elevation gain.

Access: With all of these options, there is obviously more than one place to begin your hike. For the boat-and-hike option, the trip begins from the Many Glacier Hotel. You may also begin your hike from the hotel by walking down to the lakeshore or up to the horse corral. The other popular starting point is at the Grinnell Glacier trailhead in the Many Glacier Picnic Area.

The hike: For a cool walk through the shady forest, start from the Many

Bridge over Cataract Creek on the trail to Grinnell Lake

Glacier Hotel and walk down to the lakeshore. Follow the Swiftcurrent Lakeshore Nature Trail south, up the lake. When the trail divides, stay left and walk by tiny Stump Lake and then along the forested east shore of Lake Josephine to Grinnell Lake.

The scenic traverse over avalanche slopes begins at the Many Glacier Picnic Area and follows the Grinnell Glacier Trail around the west side of Swiftcurrent Lake. When the trail divides, go right and climb a short rise, then traverse

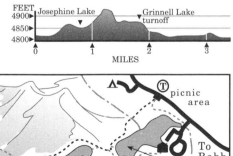

Angel Wing towers above Grinnell Lake

the west side of Lake Josephine. Views extend up the lake to Mount Gould, Bishops Cap, and Cataract Mountain. Near the upper end of Lake Josephine, bear left, following the boardwalk past the upper tour boat dock. The trail then parallels Cataract Creek to Grinnell Lake.

A third and somewhat longer route begins at the horse corral. Follow the Cataract Creek Trail to the Grinnell Lake turnoff, then descend to the lake. This route offers views of Grinnell Glacier and Lake Josephine.

Located in a deep cirque, Grinnell Lake is picture perfect. At the far end of the lake, Grinnell Falls plunges down the cliffs. The lakeshore is great for picnicking. Trout can be lured from the depths of the lake by wily fishermen. For the explorers, a rough path traverses around the southeastern side of the lake to the base of the falls.

■ ■ ■ ■

44. GRINNELL GLACIER

DAY HIKE
Round trip: 11 miles (17.6 km)
Elevation gain: 1,698 feet (518 m)
High point: 6,560 feet (1,585 m)
Hiking time: 6 hours
Hikeable: mid-July through September
Difficulty: moderate
Map: USGS Many Glacier

If you have never had a closeup look at a glacier, this hike offers the opportunity to take a look at crevasses, moats, bergschrunds, snowbridges, nunataks, ice caves, and moraines. If you have had plenty of experience with glaciers, then take this hike to enjoy the outstanding scenery.

The Grinnell Glacier is an excellent hike from start to finish. If you have limited time and energy, however, shorten the trip with a boat ride up Swiftcurrent Lake and Lake Josephine.

The boat-and-hike combination is a 7.6-mile round trip, with about the same amount of elevation gain.

Access: The Grinnell Glacier Trail begins at the Many Glacier Picnic Area (elevation 4,878 feet), located 0.7 mile west of the Many Glacier Hotel.

The hike: Begin your hike by following the Swiftcurrent Lake Nature Trail around the west side of the lake. At the upper end of Swiftcurrent Lake is a junction; go right and climb over a short hill on a paved trail.

At 0.8 mile from the picnic area, the trail divides again; take the right fork and walk along

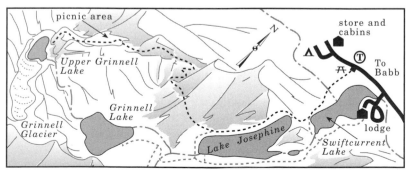

Glacier-fed Upper Grinnell Lake

the north side of Lake Josephine, with views over the lake to Angel Wing at the head of the valley. Views on this portion of the trail are expansive, and one wonders how they can improve, but they do.

Near the upper end of the lake, stay right at two junctions. The trail now begins to climb, traversing steep ledges to reach the alpine meadows on the side of Mount Grinnell. Below lies Grinnell Lake. Morning Eagle Falls comes into view below Bishops Cap, and the trail to Piegan Pass can be seen switchbacking up the rocky talus slopes of Cataract Mountain.

In the early summer, water streams off Mount Grinnell, tumbling beside and often over the trail in roaring cascades and lacy waterfalls, cooling the brow and dampening the feet.

At 5 miles is a tiny meadow with a few windswept trees. This is the site of the Grinnell Picnic Area and the end of the formal trail. From this point you must follow a rough route over the talus. It is worth the effort to scramble to the top of the moraine for a closeup view of ice-strewn Upper Grinnell Lake and the glacier.

For most hikers the lake is the turn-around point. If you must touch the ice, however, go left. Head over the rocks, creeks, and occasional blocks of ice, and pass the lake outlet to the glacier. Do not walk on the glacier: the crevasses are deep and a fall would be deadly. If you are interested in exploring the ice, do so in the company of a park naturalist. Check the schedule in the free park newspaper for the dates and times of the Grinnell Glacier walks.

■ ■ ■ ■

45. REDROCK FALLS

DAY HIKE
Round trip: 3.4 miles (5.4 km)
Elevation gain: 155 feet (47 m)
High point: 5,120 feet (1,563 m)
Hiking time: 2 hours
Hikeable: July to mid-October
Difficulty: easy
Map: USGS Many Glacier

Little preparation is required for this easy trek to a wilderness lake and colorful waterfall. This ideal half-day walk follows a wide trail along the nearly level floor of the Swiftcurrent Creek valley.

Access: From the Highway 89 junction at Babb, drive the Many Glacier Road 12 miles to its end. The Swiftcurrent Pass Trail begins at the far end of the parking lot (elevation 4,885 feet).

The hike: The trail heads into the trees, traversing a terrace up the wide, forested valley. Remember to make noise as you walk: this is prime wildlife habitat. Black bears, grizzlies, moose, and deer

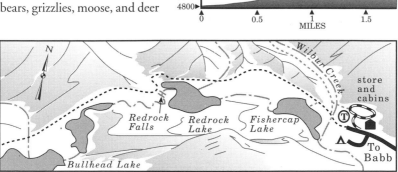

are commonly spotted from the parking lot, so sing, talk, and don't be embarrassed to query returning hikers if they have had any animal encounters.

After an easy 0.2 mile the trail crosses Wilbur Creek. Soon after, a trail descends to the left, heading to the forested Fishercap Lake, a popular area for wildlife viewing in the early morning and late evening.

Climb gradually under a leafy arbor of aspens to a rocky outcrop. From this point on the country is open and the ground cover is predominantly grass, with

Lower portion of Redrock Falls

a few mountain willows and stunted subalpine firs to add some texture to the scene.

The rounded U shape of the valley floor serves as testimony to the former power of the Swiftcurrent Glacier. At one time it swept down the valley, carving the topography to the shape we see today. Only two small sections of the once-massive Swiftcurrent Glacier remain, located in the cirques on the north and south sides of Swiftcurrent Mountain.

The trail descends to within a few feet of the shore of Redrock Lake at 1.3 miles. Although little elevation has been gained, the lake has a high alpine feel. The surrounding vegetation is low and sparse, while Grinnell Mountain soars to the horizon to the south, Mount Wilbur dominates to the north, and Swiftcurrent Mountain fills the west horizon. In the center of this high mountain scene lies the aptly named Redrock Lake. Surrounded by deep crimson rock, the lake is strikingly beautiful.

After enjoying the view from the small beach at the lakeshore, continue up the valley for another 0.4 mile to Redrock Falls, clearly visible at the upper end of the lake. At 1.7 miles, leave the trail to walk over to the falls and examine the deep, red rock rib (argillite) that gives the lake and falls their very distinctive look.

BEAR SPRAY

The so-called "bear spray" is actually canned mace or cayenne pepper spray. Although it is expensive, most hikers and many Park Service employees carry it. This product is a last line of defense and should not replace the normal precautions of making noise on the trail and walking in groups.

To be an effective defense against bears, the spray needs to be readily available. Wear it on your belt or attached to a strap of your pack. Buy the carrying case so you can be certain the attachment is secure. Practice getting it out of its case in a hurry, then practice preparing the can to fire. Above all, make sure you know how to aim it properly.

Pepper-spray rules are simple: The bear must be no more than 15 feet from you before you use it, and do not attempt to spray into the wind. (Both Glacier and Waterton Lakes Parks are known for their windy weather.)

Park visitors traveling into Canada from the United States will be asked if they are carrying bear spray. Customs officials check the can to see if it is the type allowed into Canada. To avoid hassles at the border, it is best to check the can before you buy it.

■ ■ ■ ■

46. ICEBERG LAKE

DAY HIKE
Round trip: 9.4 miles (15 km)
Elevation gain: 1,219 feet (372 m)
High point: 6,094 feet (1,857 m)
Hiking time: 5 hours
Hikeable: mid-July through September
Difficulty: moderate
Map: USGS Many Glacier

On a warm summer day, hikers crowd the shore of Iceberg Lake. They come to watch the sunlight dance across the chunks of ice floating in the chalky blue, glacier-fed waters. They sit for hours, entranced by the fanciful shapes of the floating ice and contemplating the 3,000-foot cliff that rises straight out of the lake, like a giant cathedral wall.

The trail to Iceberg Lake is very popular. The tread is wide and the grade gradual. Experienced hikers will find this an easy hike, novices will find it enjoyable, and everyone will be impressed by the scenery.

Access: From the Highway 89 junction in Babb, drive to the end of the Many Glacier Road. Just past the general store, turn right on a narrow road that winds around the motor inn's cabins. Stay left and follow the signs to the Iceberg Lake trailhead parking area (elevation 4,885 feet).

The hike: The trail begins with a couple of well-signed intersections, first with the

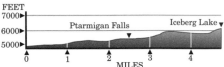

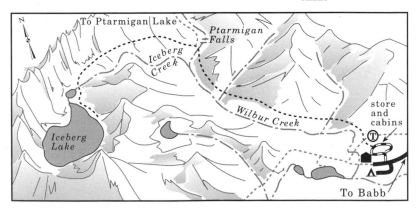

Iceberg Lake at the base of Iceberg Peak

Swiftcurrent Pass Trail (stay right), then with the trail to the Many Glacier Hotel (stay left). The Iceberg Lake Trail starts off with a steep climb, gaining 200 feet of elevation before settling into a long, gradual traverse over the open slopes of Mount Henkel. The views begin at the trailhead and before long there is a panoramic look up the Swiftcurrent Creek valley, all the way to Swiftcurrent Pass and Swiftcurrent Mountain Lookout. A profusion of wildflowers covers the open hillside below and above the trail. Bighorn sheep and an occasional bear may be seen.

At 2.8 miles the trail enters the forest and crosses Ptarmigan Creek, just above Ptarmigan Falls. Not long after, the trail divides. The right-hand trail heads up through the Ptarmigan Tunnel to the Belly River area (Hike 47). The left fork leads to Iceberg Lake.

The trail continues its traverse and gradual climb under a great barrier of cliffs known as the Ptarmigan Wall. After the forest ends at 3.2 miles, the remainder of the hike is over open slopes with entrancing views of the valley.

Cross Iceberg Creek at 4.5 miles, then climb through fragile alpine meadows for the final 0.2 mile. Rocks at the edge of the lake make excellent seats for a picnic lunch, but watch out for the squirrels that appear like magic at the same time your sandwich comes out of the pack. Don't feed these cute little creatures: our food may kill them.

■ ■ ■ ■

47. PTARMIGAN TUNNEL

DAY HIKE
Round trip: 11.2 miles (17.9 km)
Elevation gain: 2,315 feet (706 m)
High point: 7,200 feet (2,195 m)
Hiking time: 6 hours
Hikeable: mid-July through mid-September
Difficulty: strenuous
Map: USGS Many Glacier

The objective of this hike is a tunnel through the massive Ptarmigan Wall. Although this novelty may be the inspiration that gets most hikers to the trailhead, it is the spectacular scenery that motivates the legs on the long climb.

Access: From the Highway 89 junction in Babb, drive the

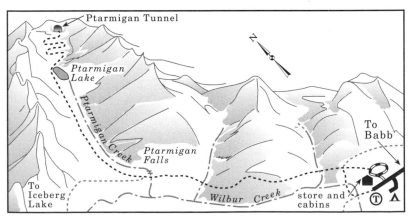

Trail ascending from Ptarmigan Lake to Ptarmigan Tunnel

Many Glacier Road 12 miles to its end (elevation 4,885 feet).

The hike: Start the hike from the end of the parking area by following the Swiftcurrent Pass Trail for 100 feet. Go right at the first intersection and walk past the Swiftcurrent Motor Inn. The trail climbs steeply at first, gaining 200 feet in 0.2 mile. In this section two more intersections are passed; stay left at both.

After the second intersection the trail begins a long traverse across the open flanks of Altyn Peak and Mount Henkel. Wildflowers, wildlife, and views all vie for your attention. Keep alert: bears frequently cross these open slopes, hunting for berries or small rodents. You also may see deer or mountain sheep on the rocks above.

At 2.8 miles, the trail enters the forest, then crosses Ptarmigan Creek at the top of Ptarmigan Falls. A short distance beyond, the trail divides. To the left is Iceberg Lake (Hike 46). Ptarmigan Lake and the tunnel are to the right.

Mount Wilbur viewed from inside Ptarmigan Tunnel

Ascend, first through forest, then across meadows with views of Ptarmigan Wall and Crowfeet Mountain to inspire weary feet. After paralleling Ptarmigan Creek for 1.6 miles, reach the end of the valley and Ptarmigan Lake. Follow the trail as it swings around the lake, then heads steadily up an open scree slope to the tunnel (7,200 feet).

No hike would be complete without a walk through the 183-foot-long tunnel to check out the view on the north side of the Ptarmigan Wall. Elizabeth Lake can be seen 2,300 feet below. Beyond lies the Belly River country, an area worth more than just a casual glance from this vantage point.

■ ■ ■ ■

48. SWIFTCURRENT PASS

Granite Park Chalet
DAY HIKE OR BACKPACK
Round trip: 15.2 miles (24.3 km)
Elevation gain: 2,315 feet in; 545 feet out (706 m in; 166 m out)
High point: 7,195 feet (2,193 m)
Hiking time: 8 hours
Hikeable: mid-July through September
Difficulty: strenuous
Maps: USGS Many Glacier and Ahern Pass

Lookout
DAY HIKE
Round trip: 15.6 miles (25 km)
Elevation gain: 3,556 feet (1,084 m)
High point: 8,436 feet (2,571 m)
Hiking time: 9 hours
Hikeable: mid-July through mid-September
Difficulty: strenuous
Maps: USGS Many Glacier and Ahern Pass

This is one of those rare trails that have so many points of interest, a short hike can be as enjoyable as a long one. Pick your destination from a list that includes four lakes, waterfalls, several vista points, a high alpine basin, a pass on the Continental Divide, and a lookout with the best panoramic view in the entire park.

Access: From the Highway 89 junction at Babb, drive the Many Glacier Road for 12 miles to its end. The Swiftcurrent Pass Trail begins at the far end of the parking lot (elevation 4,885 feet).

The hike: Heading up the Swiftcurrent Creek valley, the first point of

Granite Park Chalet and Heavens Peak in distance

interest is Wilbur Creek. Soon after is a junction with the trail to forested Fishercap Lake. The climb is gradual as the trail ascends a low rock outcrop, then heads into open meadows interspersed with mountain willows and stunted subalpine firs.

Redrock Lake, at 1.3 miles, is aptly named. Surrounded by deep crimson rock, the lake is strikingly beautiful. At the end

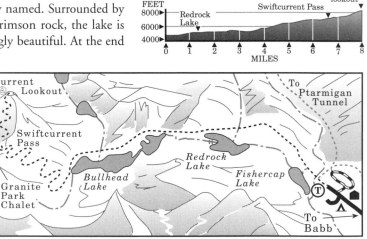

of the lake is Redrock Falls, an excellent destination for short hikes (Hike 45).

Pass a large, scenic, unnamed lake before reaching Bullhead Lake at 2.5 miles. Up to this point there has been very little elevation gain; however, just beyond the lake the trail begins to climb, gaining 2,000 feet in the next 3.5 miles.

A grassy knoll above Bullhead Lake is the first of many vista points overlooking the Swiftcurrent Creek valley. Beyond the knoll, the valley ends in a cirque, where as many as eight waterfalls could be dancing down the cliffs. The trail comes close to one of these waterfalls, then switchbacks and traverses a narrow ledge to reach a small alpine basin. After crossing a lively creek the trail divides; the old and new trails cut parallel courses into a higher basin. The final climb is through an oasis of alpine meadows.

At 6.6 miles reach the crest of 7,195-foot Swiftcurrent Pass and cross the Continental Divide. From the pass it's a 1-mile descent to Granite Park Chalet and 2 miles to the camp area. Energetic hikers are strongly encouraged to make the steep, 1,241-foot climb from the pass to the lookout at the crest of Swiftcurrent Mountain. The panoramic view is unbelievable. Two points of caution: Avoid Swiftcurrent Mountain on windy days, and do not venture too far on the north side of the lookout, where there is nothing but cliffs and a long drop to the bottom.

■ ■ ■ ■

49. THE NORTHERN CIRCLE

BACKPACK
Loop trip: 55.8 miles (89.3 km)
Elevation gain: 8,108 feet (2,471 m)
High point: 7,440 feet (2,268 m)
Hiking time: 5–7 days
Hikeable: August through mid-September
Difficulty: strenuous
Maps: USGS Many Glacier, Gable Mountain, Mt. Cleveland,
          Porcupine Ridge, Mt. Geduhn, and Ahern Pass

Hike through the wilderness of the northeast portion of the park, where more than half the trail is above timberline. This outstanding loop trail leads you from panoramic vistas to beautiful lakes, past waterfalls and rivers, to high alpine meadows and lovely fields of wildflowers.

Wildlife is abundant in the mountainous terrain traversed on this loop, and the observant hiker may see bears, elk, deer, and moose. Mountain lions roam the valleys, as do lynx. Hawks, eagles, and owls have been spotted in the forest and mountains, while numerous ducks, geese, and loons have been seen, and heard, on the lakes.

Because this is a beautiful and popular area, backcountry permits can be hard to get. Either make advance reservations or plan to apply for your permit at 8:00 A.M. sharp the day before you intend to start your hike. Arrive at the backcountry desk with two itineraries in hand, one for clockwise and one for counterclockwise. If the campsites are full in one direction, hopefully there will be space the other way.

Access: The loop begins at the end of the Many Glacier Road, 12 miles west of Babb (elevation 4,885 feet). The following description is for a counterclockwise loop.

The hike: On day one, hikers are faced with a mandatory 9.9-mile walk from Many Glacier to Elizabeth Lake, where the first backcountry campsite is located. This is a long walk for most hikers with packs bulging with supplies for the trip. From the parking area, hike to Ptarmigan Tunnel (Hike 47), then descend to find a large camp area at the outlet of the lake.

After the first day there are more campsites to choose from, and the next couple of days can be tailored to fit the time and energy constraints of the group. From Elizabeth Lake it is a gentle descent to Dawn Mist Falls. Shortly after, the trail divides. The trail to Cosley Lake is the shortest but does not have a bridge at the Mokowanis River crossing. A wire across the water provides

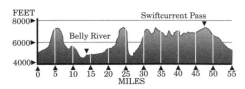

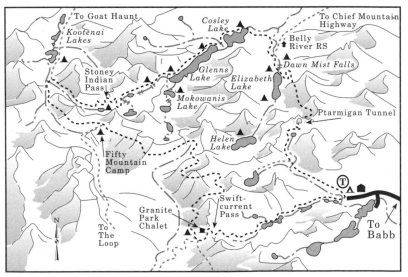

hikers something to hang on to. If you are not ready for a brisk river bath, walk down valley to the Belly River Ranger Station and head back up on the Cosley Lake Cutoff Trail. From Cosley Lake, the loop heads southwest and heads up the Mokowanis River valley to Stoney Indian Pass. At the base of Cosley Lake is a campsite; the next is located 1.5 miles up valley at the lower end of Glenns Lake, a third is located 4.3 miles up valley at the head of Glenns Lake, and just 0.6 mile beyond is the Mokowanis Junction Camp. The trail passes several small tarns, a waterfall, and a lovely cascade on its way to 6,908-foot Stoney Indian Pass, located 9.5 miles from Cosley Lake Camp.

From the pass the trail switchbacks down to Stoney Indian Lake Camp, then continues down to Pass Creek junction, 3.5 miles below the pass. The loop turns south and heads up Kootenai Creek, climbing 5.6 miles to high alpine country and to the next campsite, at Fifty Mountain. Most loop hikers will want to spend a night at this beautiful location. The next campsite is at Granite Park, 11.9 miles to the east.

From Fifty Mountain Camp the loop route follows the Northern Highline

Beargrass and Lake Elizabeth

Trail. This section is almost entirely above timberline, with the full expanse of the Livingston Range spread out for viewing to the west. The trail reaches the 7,440-foot high point of the loop on a shoulder of Mount Kipp, descends to below 6,000 feet at Cattle Queen Creek, then climbs back up to 6,800 feet by the end of the day.

From Granite Park, there are no more camp areas on the loop, so the final 7.9 miles over Swiftcurrent Pass must be completed in a single day. This last leg of the circle is relatively easy, with 1 mile of climbing and 6.9 miles of descent to Many Glacier.

If time allows try one of several excellent side trips off the basic circle, to Helen Lake, Mokowanis Lake, Kootenai Lakes, and the Swiftcurrent Mountain Lookout.

■ ■ ■ ■

50. BELLY RIVER

GABLE CREEK CAMP
DAY HIKE OR BACKPACK
Round trip: 12.4 miles (19.8 km)
Elevation gain: 80 feet in; 809 feet out (24 m in; 247 m out)
High point: 5,329 feet (1,624 m)
Hiking time: 6 hours
Hikeable: June through September
Difficulty: easy
Map: USGS Gable Mountain

Helen Lake
BACKPACK
Round trip: 27.2 miles (43.5 km)
Elevation gain: 500 feet in; 809 feet out (153 m in; 247 m out)
High point: 5,329 feet (1,624 m)
Hiking time: 2–4 days
Hikeable: July through September
Difficulty: moderate
Maps: USGS Gable Mountain and Many Glacier

Designed for backpackers by Mother Nature herself, the Belly River valley is a perfect hike with alpine scenery, waterfalls, lakes, and very little elevation gain. The lower portions of the Belly River area are snow free by June, making it an ideal early season hike. By July, the trail is snow free all the way to the stunningly scenic Elizabeth Lake and high alpine Helen Lake.

Dawn Mist Falls

Although Belly River is an easy day hike, it takes three to five days to explore this area. The longer stays allow you enough time to hike to the Gable Creek Camp and set up a base, then spend the next couple of days exploring the Belly River valley to Dawn Mist Falls, Elizabeth Lake, and Helen Lake, or to Cosley and Glenns Lakes in the Mokowanis River valley and, for the truly adventurous, visiting Gable Pass and Slide Lake.

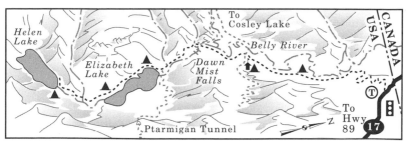

Stock fence at the Belly River Ranger Station

Before heading to the trailhead, pick up a backcountry camping permit. Permits are not issued in the Belly River area.

Access: From St. Mary, drive Highway 89 north for 12 miles, then turn left onto Highway 17 (Chief Mountain International Highway) and continue another 14.4 miles. The Belly River trailhead is located 500 feet south of the Chief Mountain border crossing (elevation 5,329 feet).

The hike: The trail begins with a 2-mile-long, 809-foot descent to the valley floor. Due to a combination of heavy horse traffic and clay soil, the trail can be very muddy after a rain. Walk carefully to avoid slipping when the trail is wet.

Follow an old wagon road up the valley through aspen groves and grassy meadows (be prepared for a lot of mosquitoes here). At 3 miles, the trail brushes the edge of the Belly River.

Continuing up the valley, cross one grassy meadow after another with views of Chief, Gable, Sentinel, and Bear Mountains. At 6.2 miles you will reach the forested Gable Creek Camp.

A few feet beyond Gable Creek Camp is a fancy wooden fence, which signals your arrival at the Belly River Ranger Station. The trail divides here. The first junction is with the Cosley Lake Cutoff Trail to Stoney Indian Pass (Hike 52). Stay left and walk across the meadow to a second junction with the trail to the ranger station and Slide Lake (Hike 51). Continue straight across the meadow then begin the long climb toward Elizabeth Lake.

At 7.8 miles cross the Belly River on a bouncy suspension bridge. A few feet beyond the river crossing, the Belly River Trail intersects an alternate trail from Cosley Lake. Head left. At 8.2 miles, a short side trail branches left, descending to the base of the impressive Dawn Mist Falls.

The trail arrives at the lower of the two Elizabeth Lake campsites and divides at 9.8 miles. To the left is the trail to Redgap Pass and Ptarmigan Tunnel. The trail on the right heads on up valley to a second, less scenic campsite at the head of Elizabeth Lake at 11.2 miles. The Belly River Trail ends at 13.6 miles in a narrow cirque where beautiful Helen Lake lies at the base of Ahern Peak, receiving much of its water and distinctive coloring from the Ahern Glacier.

■ ■ ■ ■

51. GABLE PASS AND SLIDE LAKE

BACKPACK
Round trip: 22 miles (35.2 km)
Elevation gain: 2,271 feet in; 2,129 feet out (683 m in; 659 m out)
High point: 7,520 feet (2,296 m)
Hiking time: 2–4 days
Hikeable: July through September
Difficulty: difficult
Maps: USGS Chief Mountain and Gable Mountain

Tucked away in the isolated Otatso Creek valley, Slide Lake is an ideal destination for adventurous hikers. With three radically different ways to access the lake, getting there is part of the adventure.

This rarely visited lake was once the site of a mining operation. An old, partially washed-out mining road up Otatso Creek can be traversed by mountain bike to the park boundary. At that point it is a 1.6-mile walk to Slide Lake.

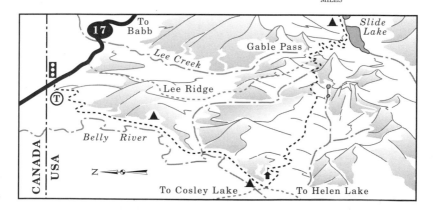

Anyone interested in this approach will need to buy a pass to travel over Blackfeet lands. In 2002, these passes, as well as driving directions, were available at the Many Glacier and St. Mary Ranger Stations.

The second access to the Gable Pass and Slide Lake area is via the rarely maintained Lee Ridge Trail. The 8-mile access is slightly shorter and far less scenic than the one described here.

For hikers, the most picturesque access is from the Belly River over the rock-studded parkland of Gable Pass, then down to the lake. This route is long, strenuous, and demands some careful navigation of the long traverse below Gable Mountain.

Access: From St. Mary, drive Highway 89 north for 12 miles, then turn left onto Highway 17 (Chief Mountain International Highway) and continue another 14.4 miles. The trailhead is located 500 feet south of the Chief Mountain border crossing (elevation 5,329 feet).

The hike: The trip to Gable Pass and Slide Lake begins with a 6.2-mile trek up the Belly River. The trail starts off with a 2-mile-long, 809-foot descent to the valley floor. Due to a combination of heavy horse traffic and clay soil, the

View of the Gable Pass area from the Bear Mountain Point overlook

trail can be very muddy after a rain. Walk carefully to avoid slipping when the trail is wet.

Follow an old wagon road up the valley through aspen groves and grassy meadows (breeding ground for many biting bugs). A rarely used and hardly ever maintained trail to Miche Wabun Lake branches right at 3 miles to ford the Belly River.

Continuing up the valley, cross one grassy meadow after another with views of Chief Mountain, Gable Mountain, Cosley Ridge, and Sentinel and Bear Mountains. At 6 miles you will encounter a fancy wooden fence, signaling your arrival at the Belly River Ranger Station. The trail divides here. The first junction is with the Stoney Indian Pass Trail (Hike 52); stay left. Go left again when you reach the second junction at 6.1 miles, then follow this trail to the ranger station. Walk around the building to find the Slide Lake Trail on the backside (4,720 feet).

The trail climbs rapidly up the forested hillside. This old-style trail

Beargrass

uses the no-nonsense approach, gaining elevation at a steady, sometimes breathtaking pace, without the bother of switchbacking all over the place. As a result of this straightforward ascent, the trail breaks out of the forest and enters the alpine world in less than 2 miles. The trail continues to climb, ascending an open ridge on the side of Gable Mountain. In some areas the trail tread disappears, leaving you to follow a moderately well-defined line of cairns. Unless you are a competent routefinder, do not attempt this crossing in bad weather when the cairns are not easily visible.

Three miles above the Belly River Ranger Station is the junction with Lee Ridge Trail (7,400 feet). Stay right for a 0.4-mile descending traverse to 7,180-foot Gable Pass. Views of three very old and eroded volcanic plugs add interest to this section of the trail. From the pass the trail descends through a boulder field, then into the forest for the final 1.4 miles to the shores of Slide Lake (6,006 feet). The campsite is located 0.2 mile down valley to the left.

■ ■ ■ ■

52. MOKOWANIS LAKE AND STONEY INDIAN PASS

Mokowanis Lake
BACKPACK
Round trip: 28.8 miles (46 km)
Elevation gain: 434 feet in; 809 feet out (134 m in; 247 m out)
High point: 5,329 feet (1,624.5 m)
Hiking time: 3–5 days
Hikeable: mid-June through mid-October
Difficulty: moderate
Maps: USGS Gable Mountain, Mt. Cleveland, and Ahern Pass

Stoney Indian Lake
BACKPACK
Round trip: 37.8 miles (60.5 km)
Elevation gain: 2,382 feet in; 1,417 feet out (727 m in; 433 m out)
High point: 6,908 feet (2,105 m)
Hiking time: 4–6 days
Hikeable: August through mid-September
Difficulty: strenuous
Maps: USGS Gable Mountain, Mt. Cleveland, Ahern Pass, and
Porcupine Ridge

This hike has it all: wide, glacier-carved valleys, high mountain lakes, wildflowers, meadows, formidable mountains, glaciers, rivers, waterfalls, vistas, and the occasional deer, mountain goat, and bighorn sheep. It is no wonder that this exceptional area is an extremely popular destination for backpackers. Advance reservations are strongly recommend if you are planning to include Mokowanis Lake or Stoney Indian Pass as part of your itinerary on your next trip to Glacier National Park.

Access: From St. Mary, drive Highway 89 north for 12 miles, then turn left onto Highway 17 (Chief Mountain International Highway) and continue another 14.4 miles. The trailhead is located 500 feet south of the Chief Mountain border crossing (elevation 5,329 feet).

The hike: The first 6 miles of this hike is on the Belly River trail (Hike 50). The stroll up the Belly River valley sets the tone for the trip: eye-catching scenery and a nearly level trail.

At 6 miles a fancy wooden fence signals your arrival at the Belly River Ranger Station. The trail divides here. Go right and descend to cross the Belly River on a suspension bridge that is removed for the winter by mid-September.

Paralleling the Mokowanis River, the trail ascends an old lateral moraine left by a glacier from the Belly River. At 7.9 miles a short spur trail branches off to the left, descending to the top of Gros Ventre Falls. At the 8-mile point the trail to Bear Mountain Point heads off to the right, climbing steeply for 1.7

Suspension bridge over the Belly River

miles to the site of the old lookout. The views from the top are worth the effort to get there.

At 8.2 miles, pass the Belly River Cutoff Trail. This trail has a cable to help hikers ford the river, but no bridge. A half-mile beyond, pass the spur trail to Cosley Lake Camp. At 10.2 miles pass Glenns Lake Foot Camp and at 12.8 miles pass Glenns Lake Head Camp. A short 0.3 mile up valley is the Mokowanis Lake turnoff.

The final 1.3 miles to Mokowanis Lake is an easy stroll around the upper end of Glenns Lake, past White Quiver Falls, and through forest and across rock to reach the subalpine lake at 14.4 miles. Surrounded by tall peaks and in sight of a large waterfall, the lake is an ideal base-camp location for day trips on up the valley.

After the Mokowanis Lake turnoff, the trail to Stoney Indian Pass soon begins to climb. After 2.8 miles pass little Atsina Lake (5,960 feet) and head into ever-broadening views. The trail continues its steady ascent, passing several small waterfalls and a couple of tarns before reaching the high alpine crest of 6,908-foot Stoney Indian Pass, 4.8 miles past the Mokowanis Lake turnoff. This is an ideal day hikers' turnaround. If camping, descend steeply for a mile to the shores of Stoney Indian Lake and camp area.

■ ■ ■ ■

OTHER TRAILS

Lee Ridge Trail is a rarely used approach to Gable Pass and Slide Lake (Hike 51). The forest trail is easy to follow, although you may have to climb over some downed lodgepole pines on the way. The trailhead is located on the Chief Mountain Highway at about milepost 17.6. A turnout/parking area is located 0.2 mile beyond the trailhead on the north side of the road.

The North Fork Trail is used to access Miche Wabun Lake. The trail begins at the 3-mile point on the Belly River trail (Hike 50). Hikers must ford the Belly River—a chilling but survivable experience in August—then follow the rarely maintained trail through the forest for 5 miles around Sentinel Mountain to the North Fork Belly River and the lake.

White Quiver Falls at the upper Mokowanis Lake trail

Goat Haunt

Long before man began recording his journeys, people have been visiting the Goat Haunt area at the western end of Upper Waterton Lake: first Indians, then trappers, next loggers and hunters, and finally tourists. The Indians came and went for thousands of years, leaving little mark on the area. European settlers, since their arrival less than 200 years ago, have greatly impacted this area by hunting the goats to near extinction and constructing a road to haul logs over the mountains.

Times change. Goat Haunt became part of Glacier National Park in 1910. For many years it was the location of a wilderness lodge built for tourists who traveled on horseback across Glacier National Park. In 1962 the lodge was swept away in a flood, and the Park Service did not rebuild. Today, neither food nor lodging is available to the visitor at Goat Haunt.

Despite the endless stream of visitors down through the centuries, the back door of the Goat Haunt Ranger Station still opens to some of the most isolated wilderness in Glacier National Park.

Mountain goat

GOAT HAUNT TRAIL FINDER

Trail Number and Destination	Difficulty	Features						
		Lowland Lakes	Alpine Lakes	Waterfalls	Scenic Views	Wildlife	Fishing	Backpacking
53. Goat Haunt Overlook	moderate				●			
53. Rainbow Falls	easy			●				
54. Kootenai Lakes	easy	●				●		●
55. Boulder Pass Trail–East Side	moderate		●		●		●	●

ACCOMMODATIONS AND SERVICES

Goat Haunt is a basic backcountry ranger station with a few extras. There is an International Peace Pavilion, where naturalists give talks and visitors can learn to identify wildflowers and animal tracks. A second pavilion provides historical insights into the area. Visitors can get trail information and climbing or backcountry camping permits at the shoebox-size ranger office. (*Note:* Backcountry permits are issued at Goat Haunt on a space-available basis. If you wait until you reach Goat Haunt to apply for your backcountry camping permit, you may find yourself heading back down the lake on the same boat you came up on. Apply for your permit before you cross the border to Canada. No Glacier National Park backcountry permits are issued in Waterton Lakes National Park.)

Two camp areas are located in the immediate vicinity of Goat Haunt and two more within easy hiking distance. The Goat Haunt shelters are located next to the boat dock. This unique camp has three-sided structures with cement floors for protection against the wind and rain. If you use a tent here, it needs to be a self-standing one.

The Waterton River campsite is located 0.8 mile from Goat Haunt on the Waterton Lakeshore Trail. This is a traditional backcountry campsite with tent sites and one food prep area. Lake Janet Camp, located on the Boulder Pass Trail, and Kootenai Lakes Camp on the Waterton Valley Trail are both within easy walking distance (less than 4 miles) from Goat Haunt.

Goat Haunt is the only entry point to Glacier National Park that is not accessible by car. The easiest way to get there is by boat from the Waterton Park townsite in Canada. The boat makes several trips every day up Upper Waterton Lake; it stops at Goat Haunt for about 30 minutes before heading back down the lake. You can, however, plan your own schedule. If you like, take the first boat in the morning, spend the entire day exploring Goat Haunt, then take the last boat back down the lake in the evening or reserve a campsite and stay a couple of days. You can also hike to Goat Haunt from several points in Waterton Lakes and Glacier Parks and catch the boat out by buying a one-way ticket, available in the townsite of Waterton Park or on the boat. The boat operates from mid-May to mid-September. Off-season visitors must use the trails.

Hikers accessing Goat Haunt from Waterton Lakes National Park, or vice versa, must remember they are crossing an international boundary. The park ranger who greets the boats at Goat Haunt is also a U.S. Customs official. Anyone arriving from Canada by boat or by foot must report to that ranger. If you hike in Glacier National Park and then cross into Canada, you must fill out a simple form and make a toll-free call to the Canadian customs officials. Carry some form of identification when you hike to avoid any problems when crossing the international border. (At publication time, a valid driver's license for yourself and a copy of a birth certificate for each minor in your group fulfilled the documentation requirements.)

■ ■ ■ ■

53. GOAT HAUNT AREA SHORT HIKES

Goat Haunt Overlook. There is an excellent view of Upper Waterton Lake and the Olson Creek valley from the crest of a knoll just east of Goat Haunt. It is a 2-mile round-trip hike with a steep climb, gaining 700 feet of elevation in 1 mile. Walk from the boat dock to the ranger station, then follow the Kootenai Lakes trail for 200 feet. The trail to the overlook begins behind the rangers' bunkhouse.

Rainbow Falls. Located on the Waterton River, the falls is an easy 2-mile

Olson Mountain (right), Porcupine Ridge (left), and Upper Waterton Lake, near Goat Haunt

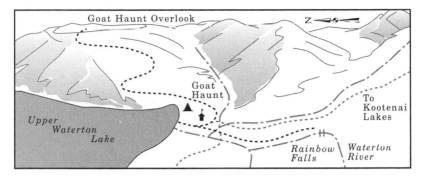

round trip with only 80 feet of elevation gain. From the boat dock, walk to the ranger station, then follow the Waterton Lakeshore Trail. After 0.3 mile the trail divides; go left and walk through the forest for another 0.7 mile to the falls.

■ ■ ■ ■

54. KOOTENAI LAKES

DAY HIKE OR BACKPACK
Round trip: 5 miles (8 km)
Elevation gain: 200 feet (61 m)
High point: 4,400 feet (1,341 m)
Hiking time: 3 hours
Hikeable: mid-May through October
Difficulty: easy
Map: USGS Porcupine Ridge

Standing about 5 feet tall at the shoulder and weighing nearly 700 pounds, the moose is an impressive mammal. Its antlers are massive, its legs are long, and each hoof covers almost as much area as the human foot.

It is the opportunity to watch moose in their natural habitat that brings so many hikers to the Kootenai Lakes area in the marshy Waterton Valley. Back-packers who spend a night at the Kootenai Lakes backcountry campground have a good chance of seeing moose in the early morning or evening hours. Moose are even occasionally spotted during the day around the lakes.

Access: Obtain your backcountry camping permit from a backcountry per-mit office in Glacier National Park, then drive north to Waterton Park town-site. Ride the boat or walk the Waterton Lakeshore Trail (Hike 58) up Upper Waterton Lake to Goat Haunt.

The hike: From the Goat Haunt Ranger Station (elevation 4,196 feet), follow

Moose

Waterton River Trail through the residential area. After a few feet the pavement ends and the trail becomes a gravel road. When the road ends, continue up the nearly level Waterton Valley on a wide trail. The valley floor is forested, with an occasional marsh and small meadows to break the monotony. At 2.5 miles go right on a spur trail to the lakes.

The Kootenai Lakes are located in a section of the Waterton Valley where the river meanders in convoluted twists and broad turns. The valley has numerous

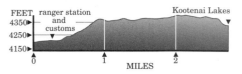

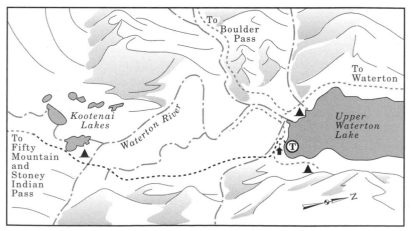

lakes, meadows, and swamps. Beavers have added more ponds and marshes. It's an altogether ideal habitat for moose. Of course, bears, deer, and elk also inhabit this lush valley. Very lucky visitors may even see a lynx or cougar.

The Kootenai Lakes are surprisingly beautiful, surrounded by meadows, the towering Citadel Peaks, and Porcupine Ridge. Animal and boot-made trails wander to several lakes—all worth exploring.

The Waterton River Trail continues up valley for another nearly level 2.5 miles to a junction with the Stoney Indian Pass Trail (4,400 feet). Stoney Indian Lake and Pass lie to the left. The pass is just 3.5 miles away and 2,500 feet higher. The main trail continues to follow the Kootenai River for another mile, then begins a steady climb along the flanks of Cathedral Peak into the alpine highlands and Fifty Mountain Camp, 5 miles west and 2,400 feet higher than the intersection.

■ ■ ■ ■

55. BOULDER PASS TRAIL–EAST SIDE

Lake Janet
DAY HIKE OR BACKPACK
Round trip: 6 miles (9.6 km)
Elevation gain: 844 feet (257 m)
High point: 5,040 feet (1,536 m)
Hiking time: 3 hours
Hikeable: mid-June through mid-October
Difficulty: moderate
Map: USGS Porcupine Ridge

Boulder Pass
BACKPACK
Round trip: 27.2 miles (43.4 km)
Elevation gain: 2,924 feet (891 m)
High point: 7,410 feet (2,170 m)
Hiking time: 2–3 days
Hikeable: August through mid-September
Difficulty: strenuous
Maps: USGS Porcupine Ridge and Mount Carter

Beautiful meadows, colorful talus, mountains, glaciers, lakes, and extraordinary vistas make this one of the most popular backcountry hiking areas in Glacier National Park.

Access: Once you have obtained that all-important backcountry use permit

Hoary marmot

from a backcountry office in Glacier National Park, drive to Waterton Park townsite and take the tour boat up Upper Waterton Lake to Goat Haunt. An alternate access is via the 8.7-mile Waterton Lakeshore Trail (Hike 58).

The hike: From the Goat Haunt boat dock (elevation 4,196 feet), walk the paved trail along the lakeshore to the ranger station, then continue on for 20 feet to an intersection. Go right on the Waterton Lakeshore Trail, and head into the forest, paralleling the Waterton River. At 0.3 mile, the Rainbow Falls

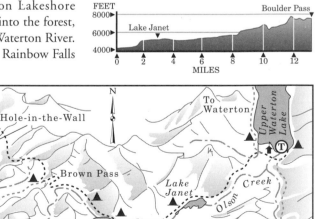

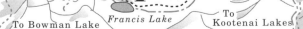

trail branches off to the left; stay on the Waterton Lakeshore Trail. Shortly after, cross the Waterton River on a suspension bridge. (The bridge is removed in the winter. Check bridge status in the spring and fall before starting out.)

Once across the Waterton River, a spur trail heads off on the right to the Waterton River Camp. At 0.9 mile the Boulder Pass Trail leaves the Waterton Lakeshore Trail and heads left, to start its long climb to the high country.

The Boulder Pass Trail ascends through forest to reach Lake Janet at 2.8 miles. The small, forested Lake Janet Camp is located just above the lake.

Views are rare in the Olson Creek valley until you reach Lake Francis (5,225 feet) at 6.2 miles. The Lake Francis Camp is located about halfway up the lake; a second campsite, Hawksbill, is located 0.5 mile beyond the upper end of the lake.

Past the lake the forest thins and is soon replaced by lush meadows. At 7.2 miles a small pond marks the start of the final push to 6,255-foot Brown Pass, which is reached at 8.6 miles. There is a campsite a short distance below the pass, on the Bowman Lake Trail.

Beyond Brown Pass, the climb continues as the trail traverses steep, open

A storm blowing in over Citadel Peaks from Lake Janet

Mule deer doe and fawn

slopes on the side of Mount Chapman. The narrow trail was blasted into the rocky hillside, and the views are tremendous. At 10.3 miles a trail branches to the left, descending to the very scenic Hole-in-the-Wall backcountry camp area.

Boulder Pass (7,410 feet) is reached at 13.6 miles, and the camp area is 0.5 mile farther on, in the basin beyond the pass.

Part Two

Waterton Lakes National Park

Waterton Park Townsite

Waterton Park townsite is the heart of the activities, lodging, services, and administration of Waterton Lakes National Park. The townsite is a busy place during the summer months, and the streets overflow with cars, RVs, tourists, cyclists, bighorn sheep, deer, and an occasional bear.

The townsite is scenically located on a small delta, sandwiched between mountains and cliffs to the north and west and beautiful Upper Waterton Lake to the south and east. And overlooking the entire scene is the majestic Prince of Wales Hotel.

With all the scenery and abundant wildlife, it is easy to disregard the one flaw in this paradise: the wind. It's a curious fact that all of the larger lakes of Waterton Lakes and Glacier National Parks are aligned with the mountains and act like funnels for the wind as it speeds from the cool and damp west side of the Rockies to the warm, dry eastern plains. This explains the saying, "The wind is not really blowing until there are whitecaps in the toilet bowls at the Prince of Wales Hotel." So come to the park prepared for wind. Although the mountain valleys offer some protection from the wind, you should pack a wind jacket, hat, and gloves when you hike to lakes or the ridge tops.

Prince of Wales Hotel overlooking Middle and Upper Waterton Lakes

Trail Number and Destination	Difficulty	Features						
		Lowland Lakes	Alpine Lakes	Waterfalls	Scenic Views	Wildlife	Fishing	Backpacking
56 Linnet Lake Loop	easy	•						
56 Bears Hump	strenuous				•			
56 Townsite Trail	easy	•			•			
56 Lower Bertha Falls	easy			•				
56 Akamina Lake	easy	•						
56 Cameron Lakeshore	easy		•					
56 Red Rock Canyon Loop	easy				•			
56 Blakiston Falls	easy			•				
56 Belly River	easy					•	•	•
57 Bertha Lake and Falls	moderate		•	•				•
58 Waterton Lakeshore Trail	moderate	•			•			•
59 Crypt Lake	difficult		•	•	•			•
60 Crandell Lake	easy						•	•
61 Goat Lake	strenuous		•		•	•	•	•
62 Twin Lakes Loop	moderate		•	•				•
63 Lineham Falls	moderate			•				
64 Rowe Lakes	moderate		•					
65 Lineham Ridge and Lineham Lakes	strenuous		•		•			•
66 Cathew–Alderson Traverse	moderate	•	•	•	•			•
67 Forum and Wall Lakes	moderate		•					•
68 Wishbone (Bosporus) Trail	easy					•	•	
69 Horseshoe Basin	moderate				•			•
70 Continental Divide National Scenic Trail	difficult	•	•	•	•	•	•	•

ACCOMMODATIONS AND SERVICES

Although the best-known accommodation in the park is the stately Prince of Wales Hotel, there are seven other motels in Waterton Park townsite. Make your reservations well in advance; all accommodations are booked solid during the summer and the nearest metropolitan center with lodging is Cardston, located 43 km east of the park. The Alberta Tourism Office is a great information resource. Contact them at (800) 661-8888, *parkscanada.pch.gc.ca/waterton*, or *www.watertonchamber.com*. If you prefer the paper-and-pen method, write to the Waterton Chamber of Commerce, P.O. Box 5500, Waterton Lakes National Park, Alberta, Canada T0K 2M0.

From fast food to formal dining, Waterton Park townsite has a wide variety of restaurants. There is even high tea served in the afternoons at the Prince of Wales Hotel. The townsite has one small grocery store with a full selection of snack food, camping food, and backpacking supplies. The prices are a bit steep.

There are three campgrounds in Waterton Lakes National Park. Waterton Townsite Campground has 238 sites; 95 are fully serviced. The campground has running water, showers, cooking shelters, and wood split and ready for a campfire. Evening programs are held at the indoor theater in July and August. The campground has a beautiful location near the lakeshore, but can be extremely windy. Do not leave your tent unattended unless it is firmly staked down.

Crandell Campground, located on the Red Rock Parkway, has 129 sites and no hookups. This area is sheltered by trees, which provide some protection from the pervasive winds. The campground has running water, cooking shelters, a play area for the kids, and split wood for fires.

Belly River Campground, located on Highway 17 (Chief Mountain International Highway), is the most primitive of the three campgrounds. It has twenty-four sites, a cook shelter, split wood for campfires, vault toilets, a playground for kids, and is an ideal area for tent campers. Most sites are sheltered from the wind.

Three private campgrounds are located near the park entrance. For details, inquire at the park Information Centre located at the Waterton Park townsite entrance.

Waterton Park townsite has two gas stations, a Laundromat, a bike shop, a sporting goods store, a bookstore, a pharmacy, photo supplies, and souvenirs galore. Money can be exchanged at the bank or you can skip the inconvenience of changing money and use any major credit card.

Pat's Gas Station rents mountain bikes as well as surreys, scooters, and baby strollers. Bring your own helmets and other riding gear. Rent canoes, rowboats, and paddleboats at Cameron Lake.

Private boats are allowed on Middle and Upper Waterton Lakes. They may be launched in Upper Waterton Lake from behind the park administration building or on Middle Waterton Lake from the Linnet Lake area, just east of the Prince of Wales Hotel. Due to the winds, the use of canoes, kayaks, or rowboats is not allowed on the upper lake.

■ ■ ■ ■

56. WATERTON LAKES NATIONAL PARK AREA SHORT HIKES

Linnet Lake Loop. This is an easy 1-km loop on a paved trail around Linnet Lake. The wheelchair-accessible trail is located adjacent to the Middle Waterton Lake boat ramp.

Bears Hump. This highly recommended hike is a strenuous 2.4-km round trip with a 200-meter elevation gain. The destination: a rocky hill with one of the best views in the park. The trail begins at the Information Centre, opposite the Prince of Wales Hotel.

Townsite Trail. This is an easy, level walk on a paved trail along the shores of Upper Waterton Lake. Pick up the trail anywhere in town and follow it as far as you want. From end to end and back again, the hike is 6.4 km.

Lower Bertha Falls. The 5.8-km round trip to the falls, with only a 150-meter elevation gain, is one of the most popular walks in the park. See Bertha Lake and Falls (Hike 57) for directions.

Akamina Lake. This is an easy 1-km round-trip hike to a small, forested lake. The trail begins at the Cameron Lake parking lot at the end of the Akamina Parkway.

Rental boats at Cameron Lake

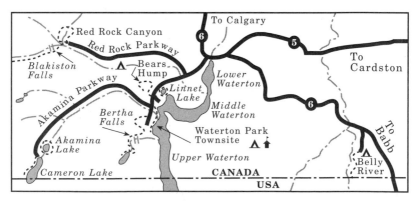

Vimy Peak viewed from the summit of Bears Hump

Cameron Lakeshore. No elevation gain is found on this easy 3.2-km round-trip walk along the west shore of Cameron Lake to a small peninsula and viewpoint. The trail begins at the Cameron Lake parking lot at the end of the Akamina Parkway.

Red Rock Canyon Loop. No one should miss this easy 0.7-km loop walk around Red Rock Canyon to view the colorful rock. The trail starts at the parking area, located at the end of the Red Rock Parkway.

Blakiston Falls. A scenic and easy 2-km round trip leads to a viewpoint of this impressive falls. The walk begins from the parking lot at the upper end of the Red Rock Parkway. Walk across the bridge, then go left.

Belly River. Starting at the far end of the group area at the Belly River Campground, an unsigned trail follows the old wagon road up valley. The entire hike is a 6.4-km round trip with only minor elevation gain. Views begin at 2.4 km, and the trail ends in a brushy quagmire near the Canada–United States border at 3.2 km.

■ ■ ■ ■

57. BERTHA LAKE AND FALLS

Bertha Falls
DAY HIKE
Round trip: 5.8 km (3.6 mi)
Elevation gain: 150 meters (429 ft)
High point: 1,435 meters (4,708 ft)
Hiking time: 2½ hours
Hikeable: July through mid-October
Difficulty: easy
Map: Waterton Lakes National Park 1:50,000 contour map
Bertha lake
DAY HIKE OR BACKPACK
Round trip: 13.8 km (8.6 mi)
Elevation gain: 470 meters (1,542 ft)
High point: 1,755 meters (5,758 ft)
Hiking time: 5 hours
Hikeable: mid-July through September
Difficulty: moderate
Map: Waterton Lakes National Park 1:50,000 contour map

Legend has it that Bertha was one of the original settlers at Waterton Park townsite. Although the very resourceful Bertha was eventually put in jail for passing bad money, there is nothing counterfeit about the excellence of this hike to a waterfall and lake that bear her name.

Both the falls and the lake are popular destinations. The hike to the falls is on a broad trail with

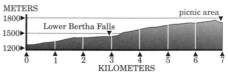

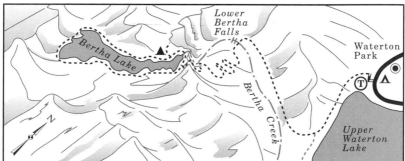

only moderate elevation gain, numerous viewpoints, and signs to explain the different vegetation. The falls are pretty, though not spectacular; the creek, however, is a popular wading and foot-bathing area.

Beyond the falls is a series of steep switchbacks. Beautiful subalpine Bertha Lake, in its deep valley, is worth the effort it takes to hike there.

Access: The trail to Bertha Lake begins at the northwestern end of Waterton Park townsite. If you are arriving by car, drive past the turnoff to the Akamina Parkway, then head through town, staying right at all intersections. Pass Cameron Falls and continue 0.3 km to the Waterton Lakeshore trailhead parking area (elevation 1,285 meters).

The hike: Begin the hike by following the Waterton Lakeshore Trail along the west shore of the lake. Views start right away, first overlooking the townsite to Bears Hump, then extending across the lake to the rocky spires of Vimy Peak.

At 1.5 km, the trail divides. Leave the Waterton Lakeshore Trail and take the right fork up the Bertha Creek valley for another 1.4 km to Lower Bertha Falls. The falls is a fascinating area. Bertha Creek is a wide curtain of water when it plunges over the cliff. Then, at the base, the water funnels together to rush down a narrow channel cut into a layer of slanting strata.

If you are heading on to the lake, cross Bertha Creek, then begin the 4-km climb up the forested hillside, gaining 320 meters. At 6.8 km the trail divides.

Middle Waterton Lake viewed from Bertha Lake

The left fork ends in 5 meters at a viewpoint overlooking Bertha Lake, Mount Alderson, and Mount Richards. The right fork descends steeply to the lakeshore. Continuing to the right, cross the outlet stream to reach, in 0.2 km, the backcountry camp area; a few feet beyond is the picnic area and beach. Those who want to explore can follow the trail around the entire lake.

■ ■ ■ ■

58. WATERTON LAKESHORE TRAIL

DAY HIKE OR BACKPACK
One way: 13.8 km (8.7 mi)
Elevation gain: 300 meters (984 ft)
High point: 1,400 meters (4,593 ft)
Hiking time: 5 hours
Hikeable: mid-June through mid-October
Difficulty: moderate
Maps: USGS Porcupine Ridge and Waterton Lakes National Park
        1:50,000 contour map

Only two trails in Waterton/Glacier International Peace Park actually cross the border between the two countries. The North Boundary Trail from Cameron Lake to Waterton Lake is one and the Waterton Lakeshore Trail is the other.

With an early start from the Waterton Park townsite, it is relatively easy to hike to Goat

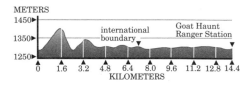

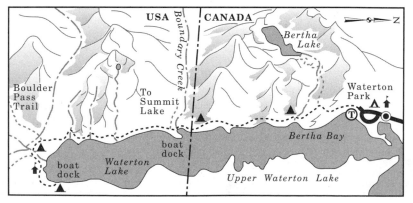

Haunt in the morning and ride the boat back in the late afternoon. This itinerary is leisurely enough to enjoy rest stops and a picnic lunch along the trail. Of course, the hike can be done in the other direction, starting with the boat ride and ending with the hike back down the lake. This second itinerary has the advantage of no schedule to follow. (*Note:* The tour boat runs from mid-May through mid-September.)

With the choice of four campsites along the lake, it is very easy to turn this trip into a 2- or 3-day adventure. (*Note:* Backcountry permits for the two U.S. camp areas must be obtained in Glacier National Park.)

Throughout the summer, a ranger from Glacier National Park teams up with a park interpreter from Waterton Lakes National Park once a week to lead hikes

Waterton Park townsite and Upper Waterton Lake

Mule deer enjoying an afternoon snack along the trail

from Waterton Park townsite to Goat Haunt. These walks are great opportunities to learn about the flora, fauna, history, and the international aspects of the park while enjoying the company of a group. Check in the free park newspaper for dates and times of these hikes.

Access: Drive to the Waterton Park townsite and park either at the Bertha Lake trailhead (see Hike 57 for directions) or at the tour boat dock. From the tour boat dock, walk south along the lakeshore trail and follow signs to the Bertha Lake/Waterton Lakeshore trailhead (elevation 1,285 meters).

The hike: The Waterton Lakeshore Trail begins as a nature walk. As the trail climbs, plaques give descriptions of the vegetation. At 1.5 km the Bertha Lake Trail and most of the hikers head off to the right. Stay left and descend to Bertha Bay, location of the first backcountry camp area.

After a brief brush with the lakeshore, the Waterton Lakeshore Trail climbs above the lake again, completing the first and most strenuous of the many descents and climbs you will make along the lake.

The most dramatic point of the hike is reached at 6.7 km, when the trail leaves the forest and crosses the 8-meter-wide swath that marks the international boundary between Canada and the United States. The second backcountry campsite is located at Boundary Bay on the Canadian side.

Walk across the border, pass a boat dock, then head away from the lake to cross West Boundary Creek at 7.2 km. A short distance beyond is a junction with the North Boundary Trail. Continue straight.

The United States portion of the trail is forested, with few views. At 12 km, a trail to the Waterton River Camp heads off to the left. The main trail turns right and heads west for 0.4 km to the Boulder Pass Trail intersection. Go left and cross the Waterton River on a suspension bridge, then pass the trail to Rainbow Falls (an excellent side trip if you have time to spare). The final 0.5 km is a pleasant forest ramble that ends at the Goat Haunt Ranger Station.

Walk the paved path along the lakeshore to the International Peace Pavilion, camping shelters, and the tour boat dock. On cool days, warm your feet at the large fire in the pavilion; on warm days, stick your feet in the lake while you wait for the boat. Visitors who are not returning to Canada that day must register with the park ranger, who also serves as a U.S. Customs officer.

■ ■ ■ ■

59. CRYPT LAKE

DAY HIKE OR BACKPACK
Round trip: 17.2 km (10.8 mi)
Elevation gain: 634 meters (2,080 ft)
High point: 1,913 meters (6,276 ft)
Hiking time: 6 hours
Hikeable: mid-July through September
Difficulty: difficult
Map: Waterton Lakes National Park 1:50,000 contour map

Crypt Lake is reputed to be the best day hike in Canada. You can expect that any hike with that kind of reputation will be somewhat unusual at the very least. For starters, the trailhead is accessed by a boat from Waterton Park townsite. The trail starts out in standard fashion, but ends with an acrobatic scramble up a ladder, a crawl through a tunnel, and a cliff-hanging ascent with the aid of a skinny cable.

This is a fun hike but not for everyone. If heights or vertigo are a problem, try one of the other excellent park trails. Younger children will have difficulties with the long steps at the entrance and exit of the tunnel. Parents who are accompanied by children may want to carry a 6-meter section of rope to secure the kids when they cross the exposed section of the cliff.

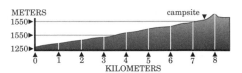

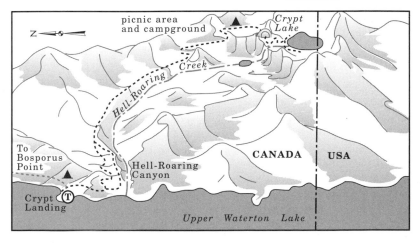

Crypt Lake trail shortly before entering the tunnel

Access: A tour boat sails to Crypt Landing in Waterton Park townsite every morning, then returns for hikers in the late afternoon. Check at the Information Centre or the Emerald Bay boat dock for the current schedule.

The hike: The trail begins at Crypt Landing (1,279 meters). From the boat dock, go right and head up a series of switchbacks that take the trail over a shoulder of Vimy Peak and into the Hell-Roaring drainage. Along the way, pass two side trails, one to Hell-Roaring Canyon and the other to Hell-Roaring Falls. These are actually two ends of the same trail. The Hell-Roaring Canyon/Falls Trail is steep and rough and makes an interesting though slightly longer descent.

In the Hell-Roaring drainage, the trail parallels the creek for 2 km. Near the head of the valley you begin to climb again, first up a hillside of colorful rocks, then across subalpine meadows.

At 7.5 km, pass through a small backcountry campsite. Horses are left here.

At this point there is only one band of cliffs between you and the lake. The trail crosses a boulder-strewn slope, then climbs into the tunnel with the help of a ladder. The tunnel is tight, so larger daypacks must be taken off and pushed through. On the far side of the tunnel, hikers must emulate mountain goats and scramble across a narrow pathway up the steep face of the cliff.

The lake is located in a cirque, just above the cliffs. The rocky shore provides an excellent location for a well-earned picnic. Ambitious hikers can walk around Crypt Lake, wandering from Canada to the United States and back to Canada.

■ ■ ■ ■

60. CRANDELL LAKE

DAY HIKE OR BACKPACK
Round trip: 4 km (2.5 mi)
Elevation gain: 100 meters (328 ft)
High point: 1,550 meters (5,085 ft)
Hiking time: 2 hours
Hikeable: July through mid-October
Difficulty: easy
Map: Waterton Lakes National Park 1:50,000 contour map

Nestled in a delicate limestone cup, the fragile beauty of Crandell Lake contrasts sharply with the massive peaks surrounding it.

Technically, this lake is more of a stroll than a hike or even a backpack. However, the lake has a cooking shelter and excellent backcountry campsites,

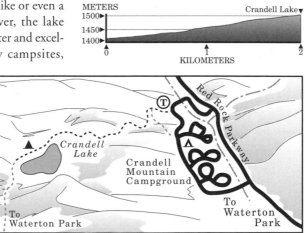

making it a perfect destination for beginning backpackers, families with very young children, or anyone who does not want to walk a long distance to spend a night in the wilderness.

Access: There are several ways to reach this lake. The access described here is off the Red Rock Parkway. A second trailhead is located in Waterton Park townsite, and another is found on the Akamina Parkway.

For the trailhead described below: From the east end of Waterton Park townsite, drive up the Red Rock Parkway 6.9 km. Go left on the Crandell Mountain Campground Road and follow it to the trailhead (1,450 meters).

The hike: The trail starts by descending along a wash for a hundred meters to reach a second trail access point from Crandell Camp, a private campground. Go left and walk through a forest of aspen and lodgepole pine. The trail varies from smooth to very rough. Watch for mountain bikes. Buchanan Ridge is visible ahead, Mount Galwey stands tall behind. After a quick 2 km a spur trail branches left and descends to the lakeshore and backcountry camp. Fishing and wading are popular activities on the pebble-covered shoreline.

Clouds boiling over Mount Crandell

■ ■ ■ ■

61. GOAT LAKE

DAY HIKE OR BACKPACK
Round trip: 12.8 km (8 mi)
Elevation gain: 530 meters (1,739 ft)
High point: 2,030 meters (6,660 ft)
Hiking time: 5 hours
Hikeable: mid-July through September
Difficulty: strenuous
Map: Waterton Lakes National Park 1:50,000 contour map

At the base of Avion Ridge lies a delicate subalpine lake surrounded by a mix of forest and meadows. The mountain goats and bighorn sheep for which the lake was named live among the cliffs and scree slopes above the lake. Hikers can fish and relax on the lakeshore or hike on the summit of Avion Ridge for expansive views across the rocky summits of the park.

Hikers to Goat Lake are likely to see mountain goats or bighorn sheep on the ridge tops and hillsides, in the campground, or even on the trail. These animals have become habituated to humans' presence and spend a portion of their day looking for handouts and human salts. Please do not encourage them. Pack out every bit of your garbage and urinate only in the facilities provided.

Access: From the Waterton Park townsite, drive east for 3.1 km. Turn left on the Red Rock Parkway and follow it for 14.6 km to its end at a large parking lot (elevation 1,500 meters).

The hike: Walk across Red Rock Canyon on a sturdy bridge and continue straight at the trail junction on the other side. Boots pound a hardened surface for a short distance, then the pavement ends and the trail widens

Hikers traversing a rocky hillside on the Goat Lake trail

into an old fire road. Follow this road up Bauerman Creek valley, through alternating meadows and forest. There are a surprising number of viewpoints from the valley floor, and Anderson Peak and Mount Bauerman put on a handsome display.

The old road makes an excellent trail for the first couple of kilometers until it reaches an open area where the bridges have washed out and two creeks must be forded. Most of the year you can hop across on the boulders. In the early summer, however, you may get your feet wet.

After 3.9 km of relatively flat valley walking, the Goat Lake junction is reached. Go right and immediately begin to climb. In the next 2.5 km the trail gains more than 400 meters of elevation. Switchbacks and steep traverses across nearly vertical hillsides take you from the valley floor to the entrance of a wide cirque in a surprisingly quick time. After passing a couple of waterfalls, the trail reaches Goat Lake at 6.4 km. Campsites are located in the meadow just above the lake.

If the spirit of the mountain goat is still within you, head on up to Avion Ridge for unobstructed views in every direction. The 1.6-km path to the ridge is considered a route rather than an official trail, which means that it can go straight up the hillside without even pretending to switchback. Once on top, the energetic hiker can walk the open crest of Avion Ridge all the way to Lost Lake.

■ ■ ■ ■

62. TWIN LAKES LOOP

BACKPACK
Loop trip: 24.8 km (15.5 mi)
Elevation gain: 650 meters (2,133 ft)
High point: 2,150 meters (7,054 ft)
Hiking time: 2 days
Hikeable: mid-July through September
Difficulty: moderate
Map: Waterton Lakes National Park 1:50,000 contour map

A basic description of the Twin Lakes Loop goes something like this: Hike up Bauerman Valley to a couple of lakes, then go over a low pass and descend Blakiston Valley back to the start. If that description fails to spark your imagination, complete the picture with views, meadows, lakes, waterfalls, a few mountain goats, and a couple of bighorn sheep.

Access: Drive up the Red Rock Parkway 14.6 km to its end (elevation 1,500 meters).

The hike: Begin the loop by walking across Red Rock Canyon. On the far side of the bridge, the trail divides. To the left is the Blakiston Creek Trail, which you will follow on the return leg of the loop. For now, go straight up the

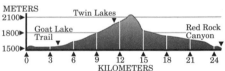

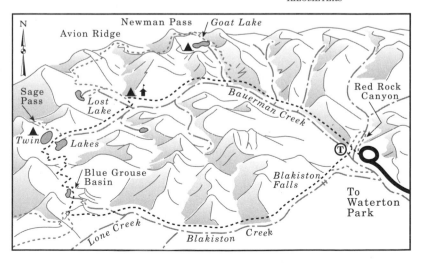

Small cascades on Bauerman Creek

Bauerman Creek Trail. After 50 meters, the pavement ends and the trail continues on an old, abandoned fire road.

Bauerman Valley is forested, with occasional open meadows and avalanche slopes where there are views of the surrounding mountains and ridges. Three creeks must be forded. Only in early summer is this a problem; generally by midsummer the creeks can be hopped with relative ease.

At 3.9 km the Goat Lake trail (Hike 61) takes off to the right. From this point, the road climbs steadily to its end at 8.4 km, where there is a small backcountry campsite, a warden's cabin, a horse corral, and a trail intersection.

Go left, cross Lost Creek, then spend the next 3.2 km climbing gradually, but steadily, to Twin Lakes. Just before reaching Upper Twin Lake, the trail to 2,140-meter Sage Pass heads off to the right. Upper Twin Lake (1,985 meters) has a backcountry camp area with a cooking shelter and stove.

The trail heads south, traversing high above Lower Twin Lake, then climbing over a low pass. This is not the high point of the loop; the trail continues to climb for another 0.5 km before descending into Blue Grouse Basin. Shortly after passing a small lake, you reach an intersection, 3.1 km from Twin Lakes.

The loop route goes left and heads down Lone Creek valley, then down Blakiston Creek valley. This section of the hike is in the forest, with only occasional views of rocky summits, 1,000 meters above.

The trail widens at 12.7 km from Twin Lakes, and suddenly you are surrounded by people who smell of fresh cologne instead of wood smoke and sweat. The attraction is Blakiston Falls. An elaborate viewing platform provides an overlook of this beautiful landmark. The final kilometer of the loop is an easy stroll on a broad trail to the base of Red Rock Canyon.

■ ■ ■ ■

63. LINEHAM FALLS

DAY HIKE
Round trip: 8.4 km (5.4 mi)
Elevation gain: 425 meters (1,394 ft)
High point: 1,980 meters (6,562 ft)
Hiking time: 3 hours
Hikeable: July through September
Difficulty: moderate
Map: Waterton Lakes National Park 1:50,000 contour map

Before you start this hike, it is important to understand what this trail has and what it has not. This trail does not have a destination; it ends in the middle of a meadow, well below the 100-meter waterfall at the end of the valley. What this trail has are views of a spectacular waterfall in a subalpine basin surrounded by the rocky walls of Mount Lineham, Mount Hawkins, Mount Blakiston,

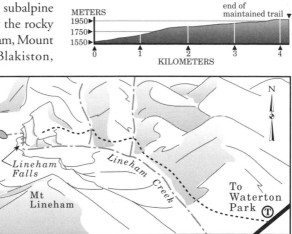

and Ruby Ridge. Above Lineham Falls are the Lineham Lakes. Many hikers have made the mistake of thinking that the falls trail offers an easy cross-country access to the lakes; it does not. Scaling the cliffs at the end of the valley requires ropes, climbing hardware, and hard hats. If you plan to climb the cliffs, check in at the warden's office before and after your trip.

Access: From the Waterton Park townsite, drive north up Akamina Parkway for 9.5 km. Park at a turnout on the right side of the road (1,575 meters).

The hike: Walk into the forest on a well-defined track. After 50 meters the trail begins to climb. With a single steep switchback, the trail ascends from the forested Cameron Creek valley to open meadows above Lineham Creek.

At the end of 1.9 km the trail reenters the forest and the climb slackens. A narrow gorge through an old moraine at 3.8 km marks the entrance into Lineham Creek basin; a small sign in a meadow at 4.2 km marks the end of the maintained trail. The two trails that continue on head to the cliffs and the climbing routes up to Lineham Lakes. Hikers who would like to continue up the valley to the base of the falls may follow either of the boot-beaten paths. When the chosen trail begins to climb steeply toward the cliff, leave it and scramble over the talus to the falls.

Open basin at the end of the Lineham Falls trail

■ ■ ■ ■

64. ROWE LAKES

DAY HIKE
Round trip: 12 km (7.5 mi)
Elevation gain: 570 meters (1,881 ft)
High point: 2,170 meters (7,161 ft)
Hiking time: 5 hours
Hikeable: mid-July through September
Difficulty: moderate
Map: Waterton Lakes National Park 1:50,000 contour map

Like diamonds, these two lakes appear slightly different every time you look at them. In the early summer the lakes lie in a setting of brilliant flowers, dominated by the white tassels of bear grass. In midsummer, the lakes take on a greenish glow, reflecting the color of the surrounding hillsides. By autumn the surrounding huckleberry fields and tamarack trees tint the water a shimmering golden yellow.

Access: From Waterton Park townsite, drive to the eastern edge of town, then head up the Akamina Parkway for 10.6 km to the Rowe Lakes–Tamarack trailhead (elevation 1,600 meters).

The hike: The trail begins with a steep climb up a forested hillside, brushing the bank of Rowe Creek at several points. After the first kilometer the climb slackens and the trail heads up the Rowe Creek valley, first through forest, then across meadows. The first junction is reached at 3.5 km. The trail on the left heads 0.5 km across the valley to Lower Rowe Lake, located at the base of a

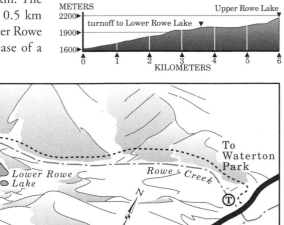

Upper Rowe Lake and Mount Rowe

cliff. The upper lake is at the top of that cliff, 235 meters above.

The Rowe Lakes–Tamarack Trail continues for another 1.2 km to Rowe Meadow and the end of the valley. The trail traverses the meadow, crosses Rowe Creek, then divides. Go left and climb the steep slope in a couple of very steep switchbacks. Along the way you will pass several well-used spur trails that are actually animal paths made by the bighorn sheep and mountain goats that inhabit the cliffs above the meadow.

At 6 km the trail reaches Upper Rowe Lake (2,010 meters). A gravel shore invites hikers to linger and ponder the drifting clouds, while meadows beckon the feet to wander among the tamaracks to the base of Mount Rowe. A very steep path climbs a shoulder of Mount Rowe to the ridge crest and views.

■ ■ ■ ■

65. LINEHAM RIDGE AND LINEHAM LAKES

Lineham Ridge

DAY HIKE
Round trip: 16.2 km (10.1 mi)
Elevation gain: 970 meters (3,182 ft)
High point: 2,570 meters (8,432 ft)
Hiking time: 6 hours
Hikeable: mid-July through mid-September
Difficulty: strenuous
Map: Waterton Lakes National Park 1:50,000 contour map

Lineham Lakes

DAY HIKE OR BACKPACK
Round trip: 19.6 km (12.3 mi)
Elevation gain: 1,020 meters in; 350 meters out (3,346 ft in; 1,148 ft out)
High point: 2,570 meters (8,432 ft)
Hiking time: 8 hours
Hikeable: August through September
Difficulty: difficult
Map: Waterton Lakes National Park 1:50,000 contour map

A windswept ridge with an incredible view and four secluded lakes are the rewards for completing this difficult hike. The trail is steep and rough. The final section to the ridge crest is more like a rock scramble than a trail. Hikers should come prepared with good shoes for the steep pitches and a jacket for protection from the wind at the top.

From Lineham Ridge it's an easy cross-country hike to the beautiful Lineham Lakes basin. Although there is no official trail, hiking boots have beaten an easy-to-follow path down the scree slope to the lakes. No official backcountry campsite has been constructed at the lakes, but primitive camping is permitted—meaning you will have to hang your food or store it in a bear-proof container. Be sure to obtain a backcountry use permit from the Visitor Centre and a list of regulations before you head out.

Access: From Waterton Park townsite, drive north up the Akamina Parkway for 10.6 km to the Rowe Lakes–Tamarack trailhead (elevation 1,600 meters).

The hike: The broad and well-graded trail begins by climbing out of the Cameron Creek valley into the narrow Rowe Creek valley. Meadows alternate

Trail to Lineham Lakes after an August snowstorm

with bands of trees until the trail reaches Rowe Meadow at 5.1 km.

The trail crosses the meadow and divides at the far side. The left fork climbs to Upper Rowe Lake (Hike 64). Go right on the Tamarack Trail and head nearly straight up the steep hillside. After 0.5 km of muscle-wrenching climbing, the trail sets off on a steeply ascending traverse over open talus slopes. Near the top, orange markers have been placed along the route to keep you from straying in low-light conditions.

The trail climbs to a well-defined saddle, then turns west to follow the ridge, away from Mount Lineham, to an unnamed crest. The narrow trail nearly disappears near the top. Acrophobes will need plenty of help or should skip the final 10 meters, where the trail sends you scrambling up bands of rock and over loose talus to the 2,570-meter high point.

The Tamarack Trail continues all the way to Red Rock Canyon; however, if Lineham Lakes are your goal, go right, leaving the trail and following the

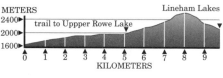

ridgeline, which descends to a saddle, then heads up toward Mount Hawkins. When you have regained about the same amount of elevation you dropped to reach the saddle, start looking for the cairn that marks the point to begin your descent to Lineham Lakes. If the trail down looks difficult, you have found the wrong one and should go back and try again. The correct path stays on the talus and avoids the cliffs as it descends to the lakes.

■ ■ ■ ■

66. CARTHEW–ALDERSON TRAVERSE

DAY HIKE OR BACKPACK
One way: 19 km (11.8 mi)
Elevation gain: 700 meters (2,297 ft)
High point: 2,360 meters (7,743 ft)
Hiking time: 7 hours
Hikeable: mid-July through September
Difficulty: moderate
Map: Waterton Lakes National Park 1:50,000 contour map

This very popular traverse from Cameron Lake to Waterton Park townsite is an ideal one-way hike. Moderately difficult, it takes you to high alpine country at windswept Carthew Pass, then descends along the shores of four high alpine lakes, traverses beautiful meadows, passes waterfalls, and crosses through deep cirques before ending at the townsite.

Hikers at the crest of Carthew Pass

The traverse usually is hiked in one day. However, if you would like to linger along the route, there is a backcountry camp area at Alderson Lake.

Access: Transportation is not a problem. A hikers' shuttle bus departs every morning from Tamarack Mall in the Waterton Park townsite; check at the Information Centre or at the sports shop in the mall for departure times. If you are traveling on a tight budget, make your way to the start of the Akamina Parkway and use your ingenuity to get a ride to the road's end at Cameron Lake (elevation 1,660 meters).

The hike: Walk past the boat

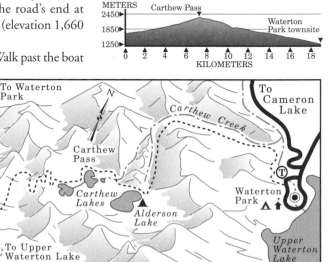

rental office and go left around the end of the lake. Shortly after crossing the outlet, the trail begins to climb the forested hillside with well-graded switchbacks. The gradual climb ends in 3.6 km at Summit Lake (1,930 meters). With a horizon line fringed with ragged summits, this lake would be a delightful destination, if there weren't so much better ahead.

At Summit Lake the trail divides. The Carthew–Alderson Trail goes to the left, climbing for the next 3.6 km to talus-strewn Carthew Pass, the 2,360-meter high point of the hike. Views from the pass are superb. To the south lies a veritable wall of mountains with two large lakes at the base, Nooney and Wurdeman.

From the pass, the trail descends on loose talus toward the three Carthew Lakes. There may be a few moments of confusion, as trails branch out in every direction. Try to stay on the main trail and avoid creating yet another path in the soft soil.

Wind around the shore of the upper lake, then descend in a couple of easy switchbacks to the middle lake. At this point the trail hops over rocks on the lakeshore, then drops out of the lake basin into a subalpine valley. Watch for

WINTER IN THE PARKS

Winter is a very beautiful time in Waterton/Glacier International Peace Park. A blanket of snow adds majesty to the towering peaks, softens the sharp outlines of the concessionaires' buildings, and creates a touch of magic in the dark, stately forests.

During the winter season the parks are covered with 0.6 to 4.5 meters (2 to 15 feet) of snow. Many of the park roads are gated. In Glacier National Park the Going-to-the-Sun Road, Camas Road, Inside North Fork Road, Two Medicine Road, Cut Bank Road, and Many Glacier Road are closed. In Waterton Lakes National Park the closure list includes the Red Rock Parkway and the upper section of the Akamina Parkway. The Chief Mountain International Highway linking the two parks is also closed. A section of Highway 89 between East Glacier Park and St. Mary is closed.

Winter camping is allowed at Apgar Picnic Area and St. Mary Campground in Glacier National Park and at the Pass Creek Picnic Area in Waterton Lakes National Park. Facilities are primitive, with pit toilets and no running water.

The main winter activities in the parks are skiing, snowshoeing, wildlife viewing, and photography. To obtain Glacier National Park's brochure, *Ski Trails of Glacier National Park*, download it from their website or write to the park and request it.

bears: the next section of the hike passes through an area favored by the local grizzly bear population.

A series of switchbacks brings hikers down into a walled cirque, skirting a monstrous crescent-shaped rock wall to reach Alderson Lake at its base, 11.7 km from the trailhead. The backcountry campsite, a picnic shelter, and an out-house are located a short distance off the main trail on the lakeshore.

The final 7.3-km stretch descends a forested valley. Just when the forest becomes monotonous, the Akamina Parkway appears on the left and, 0.8 km beyond, Upper Waterton Lake and the Waterton Park townsite come into view.

The final leg of the hike is a rapid descent along Cameron Falls. Near the bottom, the trail divides. Stay left and continue down to the end of the trail at the base of the falls.

■ ■ ■ ■

67. FORUM AND WALL LAKES

Forum Lake
DAY HIKE OR BACKPACK
Round trip: 9.4 km (5.9 mi)
Elevation gain: 335 meters (1,099 ft)
High point: 2,010 meters (6,594 ft)
Hiking time: 4 hours
Hikeable: mid-July through September
Difficulty: moderate
Map: Waterton Lakes National Park 1:50,000 contour map

Wall Lake
DAY HIKE OR BACKPACK
Round trip: 11.4 km (7.1 mi)
Elevation gain: 115 meters (377 ft)
High point: 1,790 meters (5,873 ft)
Hiking time: 4 hours
Hikeable: mid-July through September
Difficulty: easy
Map: Waterton Lakes National Park 1:50,000 contour map

Two small lakes, just west of the Waterton Lakes National Park boundary, lure hikers out of the park and across the Continental Divide to the Akamina–Kishinena Provincial Recreation Area of British Columbia. Although these two lakes are not in Waterton Lakes National Park, they are in no sense second-rate. Wall and Forum Lakes rank among the best in this area: delicate lakes in

subalpine settings, nearly overshad-
owed by towering cliffs.

No camping is allowed in the
fragile environment around the
two lakes. However, there are campsites in the valley along Akamina
Creek. Reservations are not required. The camping fee is paid to
the provincial park, not to Waterton Lakes National Park.

Access: From the east end of
Waterton Park townsite, drive
north up the Akamina Parkway for
14.5 km to the Akamina Pass trailhead (elevation 1,675 meters).

The hike: The Akamina Pass
Trail follows an old road, built in
the 1890s. It steeply climbs up the
forested hillside for 1.6 km to
Akamina Pass (1,790 meters),
which is on the Continental Divide, the border of Waterton Lakes
National Park, and the provincial
boundary between Alberta and
British Columbia.

Beyond the pass, the trail descends for 1 km to an intersection;

*One foot in British Columbia and one foot
in Alberta*

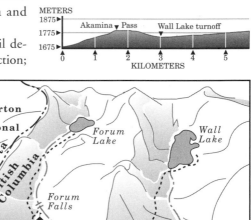

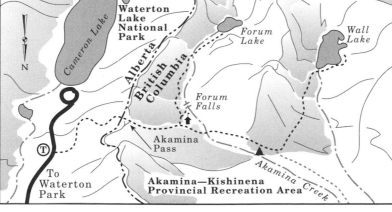

Wall Lake in Akamina–Kishinena Provincial Recreation Area

Forum Lake and the park headquarters are to the left, Wall Lake is straight ahead.

To reach Forum Lake, head left. At 0.3 km a short spur trail branches right to a deep grotto and Forum Falls. The lake trail heads nearly straight up the steep hillside, gaining maximum elevation with the least amount of trail. The climb doesn't last long, and 1.8 km from the ranger station the trail ends at Forum Lake.

For Wall Lake, continue to follow the old road along Akamina Creek from the Forum Lake intersection for another 0.5 km. At the base of a short descent is an intersection. Go left. The Wall Lake Trail contours along the forested hillside for 0.3 km, then divides. The hikers' trail goes uphill, then contours over to Wall Lake. The horse packers' trail remains almost level. Take your pick.

A high route along the crest of Akamina Ridge provides a direct and challenging connection between Wall and Forum Lakes. This route should be attempted only by experienced hikers armed with map and compass.

■ ■ ■ ■

68. WISHBONE (BOSPORUS) TRAIL

DAY HIKE
Round trip: 21 km (13 mi)
Elevation gain: 120 meters (394 ft)
High point: 1,400 meters (4,593 ft)
Hiking time: 6 hours
Hikeable: June through October
Difficulty: easy
Map: Waterton Lakes National Park 1:50,000 contour map

The Wishbone Trail (formerly called the Bosporus Trail) is an old stock route along the east side of Lower, Middle, and lower reaches of Upper Waterton Lakes. This is a scenic trail through verdant vegetation, excellent habitat for elk, moose, deer, and, of course, bear. It is an area for exploration and wilderness contemplation. Backcountry destinations include Vimy Peak and Bosporus Point.

The trail is open to hikers, as well as stock and mountain bikes. Workers who maintain this trail cannot keep up with the rapid growth of brush, and

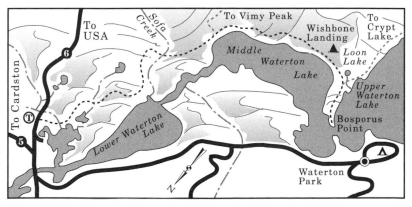

Wishbone Trail is open to mountain bikes and horses as well as hikers

the grassy meadows are frequently very wet after a rainstorm or in the morning. Gaiters are recommended if you want to keep your feet dry. This is a high bear-use area, so make a lot of noise as you travel through the brush.

Access: Drive the Chief Mountain International Highway south from its junction with Highway 5. About 500 meters south of the junction, look for a gravel turnout on the left near a gate. Park here; the trail begins on the other side of the road (elevation 1,280 meters).

The hike: The Wishbone Trail follows an old wagon road through groves of birch and aspen and across grassy meadows. Views of the surrounding mountains are excellent. In the fall, your chances of hearing the bugling call of a bull elk are better than good.

After 3 nearly level kilometers the trail drops to a large, open meadow just above Lower Waterton Lake. The wagon road ends and the Wishbone Trail heads southeast, away from the lake. In some of the wetter areas the trail is rutted and feet may get wet. At 5 km the trail crosses Sofa Creek and heads toward Middle Waterton Lake.

The intersection with the Vimy Peak Trail is reached at 6.3 km. The Wishbone Trail narrows as it skirts the edge of Middle Waterton Lake, and the tread becomes rough as it heads over a series of small ridges.

At 10.5 km Wishbone Landing Backcountry Campground makes an ideal turn-around point or overnight spot. From the campground, overnight visitors may wander over to Loon Lake or out to Bosporus Point, where horses and their riders swim the narrow channel.

■ ■ ■ ■

69. HORSESHOE BASIN

DAY HIKE OR BACKPACK
Round trip: 8 km (5 mi)
Elevation gain: 200 meters (656 ft)
High point: 1,570 meters (5,151 ft)
Hiking time: 3 hours
Hikeable: July through mid-October
Difficulty: moderate
Map: Waterton Lakes National Park 1:50,000 contour map

Hikers in Waterton Lakes National Park have come to expect broad, well-constructed trails. The Horseshoe Basin trail has neither of these attributes. It is narrow and usually brushy. However, it is the scenery that brings hikers to the area—and that scenery is excellent, with broad vistas over Lower, Middle, and Upper Waterton Lakes all the way to the United States. The objective of this hike is a rarely visited, secluded basin that just may entice you to return for even longer explorations into this wilderness area.

Access: From the intersection of Highway 6 and the road to Waterton Park townsite, drive north 1.9 km, then go left on a road signed to the Bison Paddocks. Follow that road for 0.8 km on pavement to the paddocks' entrance. Continue on gravel straight along the outside of the fence line for another 0.4 mile to the road's end. Park off the road (elevation 1,340 meters).

The hike: At the road's end, unhook the pedestrian gate, walk through, then rehook it behind you. Follow the road around the field to an intersection with the Indian Springs Border Trail.
Stay left on an overgrown road that skirts around the side of a large corral area and stick with the road as it becomes even

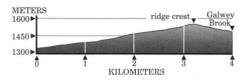

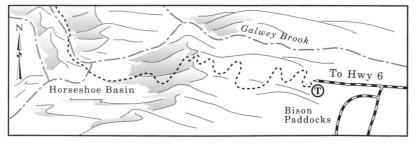

Horseshoe Basin

more overgrown and heads up the hill, the two tracks blending into one.

It soon becomes apparent that this is a horse trail that rarely sees horses. The narrow trail climbs steeply, tunneling through dense brush and thick aspen groves. Persevere: before long the trail leaves the brush and enters the open meadows. Below are miles of open, grassy hills extending east into the Great Plains and Canadian heartland. Continuing up the hillside, you will soon view Middle and Upper Waterton Lakes. At 3.2 km the trail tops the crest of a broad ridge extending off Bellevue Hill. With only minimal loss of elevation, the trail heads over the ridge and through the meadows of Horseshoe Basin to Galway Brook.

The intrepid wanderer can continue up to the crest of a 1,750-meter ridge between Lakeview Ridge and Mount Galway, then descend to Oil Basin.

■ ■ ■ ■

70. CONTINENTAL DIVIDE NATIONAL SCENIC TRAIL

BACKPACK

One way: 113 miles (181 km)
Elevation gain: 28,627 feet (8,674 m)
High point: 7,580 feet (2,310 m)
Hiking time: 10–12 days
Hikeable: mid-July through September
Difficulty: difficult
Maps: USGS Summit, Squaw Mountain, East Glacier Park, Mt. Rockwell, Kiowa, Cut Bank Pass, Mount Stimson, Rising Sun, St. Mary, Logan Pass, Many Glacier; then either Lake Sherburne and Gable Mountain or Ahern Pass, Mt. Geduhn, and Porcupine Ridge

Snaking down the backbone of the U.S., the Continental Divide National Scenic Trail travels down the spine of the Rockies, providing a hikers' link from Canada to Mexico. The Glacier National Park section of the trail is 113 miles long and more than lives up to its "scenic trail" designation.

The Continental Divide National Scenic Trail does not formally exist in Waterton Lakes National Park. That being said, many hikers choose to extend the trail by hiking the Waterton Lakeshore Trail to the official starting point at Goat Haunt Ranger Station. It has also been suggested that the Carthew–Alderson Traverse down the

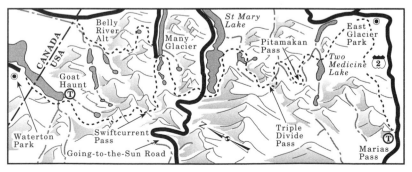

continental spine is a natural extension. Hikers need to make their own choice based on time and energy.

The Continental Divide National Scenic Trail passes through some of Glacier National Park's most loved, and most used, hiking areas. Advance reservations are strongly recommended to ensure you can follow the designated route. In some areas you can deviate from the designated route and still enjoy an excellent hike; in other areas you can't. If you have two cars at your disposal, traveling between the two trailheads is relatively easy. If you have only one vehicle, or none, call the Glacier Park shuttle service and see what they suggest.

Continental Divide hikers must traverse one difficult section of trail: the steep area along the Highline Trail between Fifty Mountain and Granite Park. Snow often lingers on the near-vertical hillsides into August and the trail may be covered with steep, hard banks of snow, necessitating ice axes most of the summer. Talk to the Glacier Park rangers before finalizing your route plans to determine if this section of trail will be open when you are planning your hike. Early season hikers—most years that includes the entire month of July—often choose the alternate route up the Belly River to avoid this hazard.

Marias Pass, on Highway 2, is the southern terminus of the Glacier National

Hikers combining their strength for a dangerous ford of a flooding creek

Mountain goat kid in a field of avalanche lilies

Park section of the Continental Divide National Scenic Trail. The northern end is at Goat Haunt on Upper Waterton Lake. To reach Goat Haunt you must either ride the lake boat or hike another 8.7 miles along the Waterton Lakeshore Trail (Hike 58) from Waterton Park townsite. The Belly River trailhead (Hike 50) serves as the alternate northern trailhead, avoiding a high-elevation traverse along the Highline Trail.

Access: Transportation between the north and south sides of Glacier National Park can be difficult. If you have only one car, leave it at Marias Pass. Park your car either at the trailhead parking area along Highway 2 at Marias Pass or at the Glacier Park Lodge in East Glacier. From Marias Pass you will need to hitch-hike to East Glacier Park, then catch the once-a-day bus to Waterton Park townsite. (Hikers planning to leave a vehicle at Waterton Park townsite will find that they must pay the daily park-use fee, which adds up quickly.)

The hike: From Waterton Park townsite, travel to the end of Upper Waterton Lake. Pass through the international customs station at Goat Haunt, then head up the Waterton valley 2.5 miles to Kootenai Lakes. Continue on another 2.7 miles before beginning the climb up a shoulder of Cathedral Peak, followed by a brief descent to meet the Highline Trail near Fifty Mountain Camp, 10.5 miles from Goat Haunt.

The next campground is located in Granite Park, reached by an extremely scenic 11.9-mile traverse. The route then leaves the Highline Trail and climbs a mile to the crest of 7,195-foot Swiftcurrent Pass before descending into Swiftcurrent Valley, passing Bullhead, Windmaker, Redrock, and finally

Fishercap Lakes before arriving in the Swiftcurrent Motor Inn parking area with access to the Many Glacier Campground, the general store, and showers. You may either walk the road to the Many Glacier Picnic Area or go left before reaching the Swiftcurrent area and its luxuries and follow forested Trail 151 down valley.

In July many hikers prefer to use the alternate trail that starts at the Chief Mountain Customs Station and heads up the Belly River (Hike 50). From Elizabeth Lake, hike over Redgap Pass, then descend to Poia Lake. The alternate route then climbs over Swiftcurrent Ridge and drops down to the Many Glacier area at the Apikuni Falls trailhead (Hike 38). The alternate route follows the main road up valley for a mile, then heads into the forest.

The main and alternate routes join together for the long haul over 7,560-foot Piegan Pass (Hike 42). After an easy descent, go left at the Cutoff Trail and continue to descend to campsites above the upper end of St. Mary Lake, 13.7 miles from the Swiftcurrent Lake trailhead. Descend gradually for the next 1.4 miles to St. Mary Lake, then go right, passing St. Mary and Virginia Falls. The trail then traverses above the south shore of St. Mary Lake for 10.3 miles to an intersection with the Red Eagle Lake Trail. Go right for another 3.8 miles to find two pleasant camp areas at Red Eagle Lake.

From Red Eagle Lake, the trail heads south up Hudson Bay Creek for 7.2 miles to 7,397-foot Triple Divide Pass. Descend the Atlantic Creek side 3.2 miles to the second junction. Go right and head up, climbing past Morning Star and Pitamakan Lakes for 5.9 miles to 7,580-foot Pitamakan Pass.

If you have time, diverge from the main route here and head over Dawson Pass to Two Medicine Lake. The official Continental Divide National Scenic Trail descends down the Dry Creek valley, past Oldman Lake, then around Rising Wolf Mountain. At 6.6 miles from the pass, go left and cross a footbridge to the Two Medicine Lake Campground.

Walk the road through the campground and pass Pray Lake to reach the shores of Two Medicine Lake. Shortly beyond the small ranger station reach Two Medicine Road. Go left and walk up the road 0.2 mile to the Scenic Point trailhead. The trail climbs 3.1 miles to a high point and descends 7.1 miles to a trailhead at the upper end of the Glacier Park Lodge golf course on the outskirts of the town of East Glacier Park (4,795 feet).

Following the Continental Divide National Scenic Trail signs, continue south 7.3 miles on the Autumn Creek Trail. Go left and in 0.5 mile pass Three Bears Lake. Just 0.5 mile beyond, the trail reaches Highway 2 and Marias Pass (5,216 feet).

Hiker on Continental Divide Trail, south of Piegan Pass

Trail Reference Chart

How to use this chart:

- Each row starts with the hike **reference number**. The **destination** is the objective of the hike.

- **Round-trip** or **loop-trip** mileage notes the entire distance that must be walked to reach the objective and return to the starting point.

- **Elevation gain** indicates how much the trail climbs to reach the destination and return to the start.

- **Hiking time** is the average time it takes the typical hiker to reach the objective and return to the trailhead. This does not include time out for birdwatching, banquets, or siestas.

- **Difficulty** is an arbitrary category and should be used with the round-trip mileage and elevation gain to determine if the hike is appropriate for your needs. *Easy* trails have little elevation gain. They tend to be wide with few or no obstacles. *Moderate* trails are well maintained and well graded. Most national park trails fall into this category. *Strenuous* hikes include steep trails or trails that spend many miles on unrelenting climbs. These hikes are physically demanding and may require experience and good sense to complete safely. Only a couple of hikes in this book have received a *difficult* rating. Only experienced hikers should attempt these routes. Challenges on these trails may include fording rivers and routefinding.

TRAIL REFERENCE CHART

Hike Number and Destination	Round-trip or Loop-trip Mileage	Elevation Gain	Hiking Time	Hiking Season	Difficulty
1 Trail of the Cedars	0.8 mi	None	30 min	June through Oct	easy
1 Fish Lake	4.8 mi	1,000 ft	3 hrs	July through Sept	moderate
1 Huckleberry Mtn Nature Loop	0.6 mi	150 ft	45 min	June through mid-Oct	moderate
1 Rocky Point	2 mi	200 ft	1 hr	Mid-June through Oct	easy
1 Howe Lake	4 mi	240 ft	2 hrs	mid-June through Oct	easy
2 Apgar Lookout	5.6 mi	1,856 ft	3 hrs	July through Sept	moderate

Hike Number and Destination	Round-trip or Loop-trip Mileage	Elevation Gain	Hiking Time	Hiking Season	Difficulty
3 Lincoln Lake	16 mi	2,407 ft	8 hrs	July through Sept	moderate
4 Mount Brown Lookout	10.6 mi	4,300 ft	7 hrs	mid-July through Sept	strenuous
5 Snyder Lakes	8.6 mi	2,035 ft	5 hrs	mid-July through Sept	moderate
6 Sperry Chalet	13.6 mi	3,240 ft	2 to 3 days	Aug through Sept	moderate
7 Sacred Dancing Cascade Loop	5 mi	200 ft	3 hrs	July through mid-Oct	easy
8 Trout Lake	7 mi	3,300 ft	5 hrs	mid-June through mid-Oct	moderate
8 Arrow Lake	13.2 mi	3,400 ft	2 days	mid-June through mid-Oct	moderate
9 Avalanche Lake	4 mi	560 ft	3 hrs	July through Sept	easy
10 Lake McDonald Trail	9.2 mi	150 ft	5 hrs	mid-June through mid-Oct	easy
11 Logging Lake Trail	10 mi	387 ft	5 hrs	mid-June through Sept	easy
11 Grace Lake	25.6 mi	577 ft	2 to 4 days	July through Sept	easy
12 Akokala Lake	11.4 mi	1,620 ft	5 hrs	mid-June through Sept	moderate
13 Bowman Lake Campground	13.6 mi	100 ft	7 hrs	mid-June through Sept	easy
13 Brown Pass	27.6 mi	2,225 ft	2 to 3 days	mid-July through mid-Sept	moderate
14 Numa Ridge Lookout	11.4 mi	2,930 ft	6 hrs	mid-July through Sept	moderate
15 Quartz Lakes Loop	12.8 mi	2,279 ft	7 hrs	mid-June through Sept	moderate
16 Kintla Lake Camp	12.6 mi	160 ft	6 hrs	mid-June through Sept	easy
16 Boulder Pass	35.4 mi	3,462 ft	3 to 4 days	Aug through mid-Sept	moderate
17 Ole Creek	1 mi	50 ft	½ hr	mid-May through Oct	easy
18 Nyack to Coal Creek	39.9 mi	2,590 ft	4 to 6 days	Aug through Sept	difficult
19 Scalplock Mountain Lookout	9 mi	3,199 ft	6 hrs	mid-July through Sept	moderate
20 Elk Mountain	7.5 mi	3,355 ft	6 hrs	mid-July through Sept	strenuous
21 Running Eagle Falls	0.6 mi	none	½ hr	June through Oct	easy
21 Paradise Point	1.2 mi	100 ft	1 hr	June through Oct	easy
21 Aster Falls	2.4 mi	100 ft	1½ hrs	mid-June through mid-Oct	easy

Hike Number and Destination	Round-trip or Loop-trip Mileage	Elevation Gain	Hiking Time	Hiking Season	Difficulty
21 Twin Falls	1.8 mi	none	1½ hrs	mid-June through Sept	easy
22 Scenic Point	6.2 mi	2,262 ft	4 hrs	July through Sept	moderate
23 Two Medicine Lake Circuit	7.2 mi	276 ft	4 hrs	July through mid-Oct	easy
24 Cobalt Lake	11.4 mi	1,406 ft	6 hrs	mid-July through Sept	moderate
24 Lake Isabel	14.1 mi	6,136 ft	2 days	mid-July through Sept	strenuous
25 Upper Two Medicine Lake	9.4 mi	370 ft	5 hrs	July through mid-Oct	easy
26 Dawson Pass Loop	15.4 mi	2,916 ft	2 to 3 days	Aug through Sept	strenuous
27 Firebrand Pass	9.4 mi	1,867 ft	5 hrs	July through mid-Oct	moderate
28 Triple Divide Pass	14 mi	2,227 ft	7 hrs	mid-July through Sept	strenuous
29 Sun Point	1 mi	30 ft	½ hr	June through mid-Oct	easy
29 St. Mary Falls	1.6 mi	300 ft	1 hr	June through Sept	easy
29 Sunrift Gorge	200 ft	100 ft	½ hr	June through Sept	easy
30 Red Eagle Lake	15.4 mi	300 ft	7 hrs	mid-June through mid-Oct	easy
31 Otokomi Lake	10 mi	1,900 ft	6 hrs	mid-July through Sept	moderate
32 Virginia Falls	6 mi	300 ft	3 hrs	July through Sept	easy
33 Gunsight Lake	12.6 mi	1,040 ft	6 hrs	July through Sept	moderate
33 Gunsight Pass to Lake McDonald	19.8 mi	3,966 ft	2 to 3 days	Aug through Sept	strenuous
34 Siyeh Pass	9.4-mi	2,390 ft	6 hrs	mid-July through mid-Sept	strenuous
35 Piegan Pass	8.8 mi	1,720 ft	4 hrs	mid-July through Sept	moderate
36 Hidden Lake Overlook	3 mi	480 ft	1½ hrs	mid-July through Sept	moderate
36 Hidden Lake	6 mi	1,235 ft	4 hrs	mid-July through Sept	moderate
37 Granite Park	15.2 mi	800 ft	8 hrs	mid-July through Sept	strenuous
37 Garden Wall to The Loop	11.8 mi one way	800 ft	7 hrs	mid-July through Sept	strenuous
38 Apikuni Falls	1.6 mi	880 ft	1 hr	July through Sept	moderate

Hike Number and Destination	Round-trip or Loop-trip Mileage	Elevation Gain	Hiking Time	Hiking Season	Difficulty
38 Swiftcurrent Lake	2.4 mi	50 ft	1½ hrs	June through Sept	easy
38 Lake Josephine	2 mi	80 ft	1½ hrs	mid-June through Sept	easy
38 Fishercap Lake	0.5 mi	100 ft	½ hr	mid-June through Sept	easy
38 Ptarmigan Falls	5 mi	500 ft	3 hrs	July through Sept	moderate
39 Swiftcurrent Ridge Lake	7.5 mi	1,332 ft	4 hrs	June through mid-Oct	moderate
40 Poia Lake to Redgap Pass Loop	27.9 mi	10,552 ft	2 to 3 days	late July through Sept	strenuous
41 Cracker Lake	11.2 mi	1,140 ft	6 hrs	mid-July through Sept	moderate
42 Cataract Creek Trail	16.6 mi	2,682 ft	8 hrs	Aug through mid-Sept	strenuous
43 Grinnell Lake	6.8 mi	272 ft	4 hrs	July through mid-Oct	easy
44 Grinnell Glacier	11 mi	1,698 ft	6 hrs	mid-July through Sept	moderate
45 Redrock Falls	3.4 mi	155 ft	2 hrs	July through mid-Oct	easy
46 Iceberg Lake	9.4 mi	1,219 ft	5 hrs	mid-July through Sept	moderate
47 Ptarmigan Tunnel	11.2 mi	2,315 ft	6 hrs	mid-July through mid-Sept	strenuous
48 Swiftcurrent Pass and Granite Park	15.2 mi	2,860 ft	8 hrs	mid-July through Sept	strenuous
48 Swiftcurrent Lookout	15.6 mi	3,556 ft	9 hrs	mid-July through mid-Sept	strenuous
49 The Northern Circle	55.8 mi	8,108 ft	5 to 7 days	Aug through mid-Sept	strenuous
50 Belly River Campground	12.4 mi	889 ft	6 hrs	June through Sept	easy
50 Belly River to Helen Lake	27.2 mi	1,309 ft	2 to 4 days	July through Sept	moderate
51 Gable Pass and Slide Lake	22 mi	4,400 ft	2 to 4 days	July through Sept	difficult
52 Mokowanis Lake	28.8 mi	1,243 ft	3 to 5 days	mid-June through mid-Oct	moderate
52 Stoney Indian Lake	37.8 mi	3,799 ft	4 to 6 days	Aug through mid-Sept	strenuous
53 Goat Haunt Overlook	2 mi	700 ft	1 hr	July through Sept	moderate

Hike Number and Destination	Round-trip or Loop-trip Mileage	Elevation Gain	Hiking Time	Hiking Season	Difficulty
53 Rainbow Falls	2 mi	80 ft	1 hr	mid-June through Sept	easy
54 Kootenai Lakes	5 mi	200 ft	3 hrs	mid-May through Oct	easy
55 Boulder Pass Trail to Lake Janet	6 mi	844 ft	3 hrs	mid-June through mid-Oct	moderate
55 Boulder Pass	26.4 mi	2,924 ft	2 to 3 days	Aug through mid-Sept	strenuous
56 Linnet Lake Loop	1 km	none	½ hr	May through Oct	easy
56 Bears Hump	2.4 km	200 m	2 hrs	June through Sept	strenuous
56 Townsite Trail	6.4 km	none	3 hrs	May through Sept	easy
56 Lower Bertha Falls	5.8 km	150 m	2 hrs	June through Sept	moderate
56 Akamina Lake	1 km	none	½ hr	July through Sept	easy
56 Cameron Lakeshore	3.2 km	none	1 hr	July through Sept	easy
56 Red Rock Canyon Loop	0.7 km	20 m	½ hr	July through Sept	easy
56 Blakiston Falls	2 km	100 m	1½ hrs	July through Sept	easy
56 Belly River	6.4 km	100 m	2 hrs	July through Sept	moderate
57 Bertha Lake	13.8 km	470 m	5 hrs	mid-July through Sept	moderate
58 Waterton Lakeshore Trail	13.8 km one way	300 m	5 hrs	mid-June through mid-Oct	moderate
59 Crypt Lake	17.2 km	634 m	6 hrs	mid-July through Sept	difficult
60 Crandell Lake	4 km	100 m	2 hrs	July through mid-Oct	easy
61 Goat Lake	12.8 km	530 m	5 hrs	mid-July through Sept	moderate
62 Twin Lakes Loop	24.8 km	650 m	2 days	mid-July through Sept	moderate
63 Lineham Falls	8.4 km	425 m	3 hrs	July through Sept	moderate
64 Rowe Lakes	12 km	570 m	5 hrs	mid-July through Sept	moderate
65 Lineham Ridge	16.2 km	970 m	6 hrs	mid-July through mid-Sept	strenuous
65 Lineham Lakes	19.6 km	1,370 m	8 hrs	Aug through Sept	difficult
66 Carthew–Alderson Traverse	19 km one way	700 m	7 hrs	mid-July through Sept	moderate
67 Forum Lake	9.4 km	335 m	4 hrs	mid-July through Sept	moderate
67 Wall Lake	11.4 km	115 m	4 hrs	mid-July through Sept	easy

Hike Number and Destination	Round-trip or Loop-trip Mileage	Elevation Gain	Hiking Time	Hiking Season	Difficulty
68 Wishbone Trail	21 km	120 m	6 hrs	June through Oct	easy
69 Horseshoe Basin	8 km	200 m	3 hrs	July through mid-Oct	moderate
70 Continental Divide National Scenic Trail	113 mi one way	15,561 ft	10 to 12 days	mid-July through Sept	difficult

Appendix: Useful Addresses

GLACIER NATIONAL PARK

General Information

Parks Superintendent
Glacier National Park
West Glacier, MT 59936
Phone: (406) 888-5441
TDD: (406) 888-5790
www.nps.gov/glac/

Glacier Park, Inc.
106 Cooperative Way, Suite 104
Kalispell, MT 59901
Phone: (406) 892-2525
info@glacierparkinc.com

Guided Trips

Glacier Wilderness Guides
Box 330
West Glacier, MT 59936
Phone: (800) 521-RAFT

Horseback Riding

Glacier Park Outfitters, Inc.
(Mid-September through mid-May)
8320 Hazel Avenue
Orangevale, CA 95662

(Rest of the year)
Many Glacier Stable
Box 295
Babb, MT 59411

Lodging

To reserve a campsite at Glacier National Park, call (800) 365-CAMP. For other overnight options, see below.

Brownies Grocery and Hostel
Box 229
East Glacier Park, MT 59434
Phone: (406) 226-4426

Granite Park Chalet
c/o Glacier Wilderness Guides
P.O. Box 330
West Glacier, MT 59936
Phone: (800) 521-7238
www.glacierguides.com

North Fork Hostel
P.O. Box 1
Polebridge, MT 59928
Phone: (406) 888-5241

Sperry Chalet
c/o Belton Chalets, Inc.
P.O. Box 188
West Glacier, MT 59936
Phone: (888) 345-2649
www.ptinet.net/sperrychalet

Transportation Around the Park

Glacier Park Reservations—Red Buses, park tours, hiker shuttles
106 Cooperative Way, Suite 104
Kalispell, MT 59901
Phone: (406) 892-2525
info@glacierparkinc.com

WATERTON LAKES NATIONAL PARK

General Information

Alberta Tourism
Phone: (800) 661-1222
parkscanada.pch.gc.ca/waterton

Waterton Chamber of Commerce
Waterton Park, AB T0K 2M0
Phone: (403) 859-2203
www.watertonchamber.com

Superintendent
Waterton Lakes National Park
Waterton Park, AB T0K 2M0
Phone: (403) 859-2224

Lodging

Waterton Park International Hostel
P.O. Box 4
Waterton Lakes National Park,
AB T0K 2M0
Phone: (888) 985-6343
(403) 859-2150
*www.watertonlakeslodge.com/
hostel.html*

Horseback Riding

Alpine Stables
Waterton Lakes National Park
P.O. Box 53
Waterton Park, AB T0K 2M0

Index

About the Authors

VICKY SPRING and TOM KIRKENDALL are both professional landscape photographers. They travel the hills with their kids in summer, with medium- and large-format cameras on their backs, looking for exotic and exquisite mountain scenery. When the snow falls, they step into cross-country skis and continue adding to their expansive collection of photos. Both Tom and Vicky studied at the Brooks Institute of Photography in Santa Barbara, California. Along the way they decided to share their extensive knowledge of scenic mountain trails to entice others to help protect these sacred places from exploitation.

THE MOUNTAINEERS, founded in 1906, is a nonprofit outdoor activity and conservation club, whose mission is "to explore, study, preserve, and enjoy the natural beauty of the outdoors . . . ." Based in Seattle, Washington, the club is now the third-largest such organization in the United States, with 15,000 members and five branches throughout Washington State.

The Mountaineers sponsors both classes and year-round outdoor activities in the Pacific Northwest, which include hiking, mountain climbing, ski-touring, snowshoeing, bicycling, camping, kayaking and canoeing, nature study, sailing, and adventure travel. The club's conservation division supports environmental causes through educational activities, sponsoring legislation, and presenting informational programs. All club activities are led by skilled, experienced volunteers who are dedicated to promoting safe and responsible enjoyment and preservation of the outdoors.

If you would like to participate in these organized outdoor activities or the club's programs, consider a membership in The Mountaineers. For information and an application, write or call The Mountaineers, Club Headquarters, 300 Third Avenue West, Seattle, WA 98119; (206) 284-6310.

The Mountaineers Books, an active, nonprofit publishing program of the club, produces guidebooks, instructional texts, historical works, natural history guides, and works on environmental conservation. All books produced by The Mountaineers Books fulfill the club's mission.

Send or call for our catalog of more than 500 outdoor titles:

The Mountaineers Books
1001 SW Klickitat Way, Suite 201
Seattle, WA 98134
(800) 553-4453
mbooks@mountaineersbooks.org
www.mountaineersbooks.org

The Mountaineers Books is proud to be a corporate sponsor of Leave No Trace, whose mission is to promote and inspire responsible outdoor recreation through education, research, and partnerships. The Leave No Trace program is focused specifically on human-powered (nonmotorized) recreation.

Leave No Trace strives to educate visitors about the nature of their recreational impacts, as well as offer techniques to prevent and minimize such impacts. Leave No Trace is best understood as an educational and ethical program, not as a set of rules and regulations.

For more information, visit *www.LNT.org*, or call (800) 332-4100.

Other Books

Available at fine bookstores and outdoor stores, by phone at (800) 553-4453, or on the Web at *www.mountaineersbooks.org*

100 Hikes in™ the Inland Northwest, 2nd Edition by Rich Landers and the Spokane Mountaineers. $16.95 paperbound. 0-89886-908-0.

100 Best Cross-Country Ski Trails in Washington, 3rd Edition by Vicky Spring and Tom Kirkendall. $16.95 paperbound. 0-89886-806-8.

Bicycling the Pacific Coast: A Complete Route Guide, Canada to Mexico, 3rd Edition by Vicky Spring and Tom Kirkendall. $14.95 paperbound. 0-89886-562-X.

An Outdoor Family Guide to Washington's National Parks & Monuments by Vicky Spring and Tom Kirkendall. $16.95 paperbound. 0-89886-552-2.

Hiking the Great Northwest, 2nd Edition by Ira Spring, Harvey Manning, and Vicky Spring. $16.95 paperbound. 0-89886-591-3.

A Waterfall Lover's Guide to the Pacific Northwest: Where to Find Hundreds of Spectacular Waterfalls in Washington, Oregon, and Idaho, 3rd Edition by Gregory Plumb. $14.95 paperbound. 0-89886-593-X.

Paddle Routes of the Inland Northwest: 50 Flatwater and Whitewater Trips for Canoe & Kayak by Rich Landers and Dan Hansen. $14.95 paperbound. 0-89886-556-5.

100 Classic Hikes in™ Washington by Ira Spring and Harvey Manning. $19.95 paperback. 0-89886-586-7.

More Everyday Wisdom: Trail-Tested Advice from the Experts by Karen Berger. $16.95 paperbound. 0-89886-899-8.

More Backcountry Cooking: Moveable Feasts by the Experts by Dorcas Miller. $16.95 paperbound. 0-89886-900-5.

Don't Get Sick: The Hidden Dangers of Camping and Hiking by Buck Tilton, M.S., and Rick Bennett, Ph.D. $8.95 paperbound. 0-89886-854-8.

Northwest Trees by Stephen F. Arno and Ramona P. Hammerly. $14.95 paperbound. 0-916890-50-3.

Northwest Mountain Weather: Understanding and Forecasting for the Backcountry User by Jeff Renner. $10.95 paperbound. 0-89886-297-3.

Staying Found: The Complete Map & Compass Handbook, 3rd Edition by June Fleming. $12.95 paperbound. 0-89886-785-1.

GPS Made Easy: Using Global Positioning Systems in the Outdoors, 3rd Edition by Lawrence Letham. $14.95 paperbound. 0-89886-802-5.

First Aid: A Pocket Guide, 4th Edition by Christopher Van Tilburg, M.D. $3.50 paperbound. 0-89886-719-3.

Emergency Survival: A Pocket Guide by Christopher Van Tilburg, M.D. $3.50 paperbound. 0-89886-768-1.